The Supporters' Guide to Welsh Football 1994

EDITOR
John Robinson

First Edition

CONTENTS

British Library Cataloguing in Publication Data
A catalogue record for this book is available from the British Library
ISBN 0-947808-28-0

Copyright © 1993; SOCCER BOOK PUBLISHING LTD. (0472-696226)
72, St. Peters' Avenue, Cleethorpes, Sth. Humberside, DN35 8HU, England

Printed by Adlard Print & Typesetting Services, The Old School, The Green, Ruddington, Notts. NG11 6HH

FOREWORD

Following the successful launch of a separate 'Supporters' Guide to Scottish Football' last year, as personal followers of Welsh Football, we were very keen to publish a similar book for Wales.

The launch last year of the Konica League of Wales has provided the impetus for a resurgence of the game in Wales and the excellent form of the national team helps too!

Our thanks go to Adrian Dumphy and Dave Collins of the Welsh Football Magazine for their tremendous assistance in the compilation of this guide and, of course, to the many club officials who have taken so much trouble to provide much of the information. Our thanks also go to Darren Kirk (cover artwork) and Michael Robinson (page layouts).

We apologise to Welsh-speaking fans as it has not proved practicable (because of lack of space) for us to include Welsh-language within the guide.

Supporters of Football League Clubs, Scottish Football and English Non-League Football should note that we publish THE SUPPORTERS' GUIDE TO PREMIER & FOOTBALL LEAGUE CLUBS -1994 EDITION (£4.99), THE SUPPORTERS' GUIDE TO SCOTTISH FOOTBALL - 1994 EDITION (£4.99) and THE SUPPORTERS' GUIDE TO NON-LEAGUE FOOTBALL - 1994 EDITION (£4.99) all of which are available, post free, from the address opposite.

Finally, we would like to wish our readers a happy and safe spectating season.

John Robinson
EDITOR

CARDIFF CITY FC

Founded: 1899	**Record Attendance**: 61,566 (14/10/61)
Turned Professional: 1910	**Colours**: Shirts - Blue
Limited Company: 1910	Shorts - White
Admitted to League: 1920	**Telephone No.**: (0222) 398636
Former Name(s): Riverside FC (1899-1910)	**Ticket Information**: (0222) 398636
Nickname: 'Bluebirds'	**Pitch Size**: 112 × 76yds
Ground: Ninian Park, Sloper Road,	**Ground Capacity**: 21,403
Cardiff, CF1 8SX	**Seating Capacity**: 5,563

GENERAL INFORMATION

Supporters Club Administrator:
Mr. M. Lambert
Address: c/o 26 Glynne St. Canton, Cardiff, South Glamorgan
Telephone Number: (0222) 398636
(messages only)
Car Parking: Sloper Road & Street Parking
Coach Parking: Sloper Road (Adjacent)
Nearest Railway Station: Cardiff Central (1 mile)
Nearest Bus Station: Cardiff Central
Club Shop:
Opening Times: Weekdays 9.00-5.00
& Matchdays 1.5 hours before kick-off
Telephone No.: (0222) 398636
Postal Sales: Yes
Nearest Police Station: Cowbridge Road East Cardiff (1 mile)
Police Force: South Wales
Police Telephone No.: (0222) 222111

GROUND INFORMATION

Away Supporters' Entrances: Grangetown End, Canton Road
Away Supporters' Sections: Grangetown End (Open)

DISABLED SUPPORTERS INFORMATION

Wheelchairs: Accommodated in Canton Stand/ Popular Bank Corner
Disabled Toilets: None
The Blind: No Special Facilities

ADMISSION INFO (1993/94 PRICES)

Adult Standing: Between £4.00 & £6.00
Adult Seating: Between £6.00 & £9.00
Child Standing: £2.00 - £4.00
Child Seating: £4.00 - £5.00
Programme Price: £1.00
FAX Number: (0222) 341148
Note : Adult prices vary depending on League position

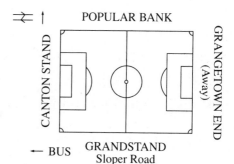

Travelling Supporters Information:

Routes: From North: Take A470 until Junction with Cardiff Bypass. Then 3rd exit at Roundabout A48 to Port Talbot, after 2 miles take 1st exit at Roundabout A4161 (Cowbridge Road). Turn right (0.5 mile), Lansdowne Road to Crossroads, turn right into Leckwith Road, then turn left (0.25 mile) into Sloper Road. From East: Exit M4 taking A48 to Cardiff Bypass (then as North). From West: Take A4161 Cowbridge Road (then as North).
Bus Services: Service No.2 - City Centre to Ground and Service No.1

SWANSEA CITY FC

Founded: 1900	**Record Attendance**: 32,796 (17/2/68)
Turned Professional: 1912	**Colours**: Shirts - White
Limited Company: 1912	Shorts - White
Admitted to League: 1920	**Telephone No.**: (0792) 474114
Former Name(s): Swansea Town FC	**Ticket Information**: (0792) 474114
(1900-1970)	**Pitch Size**: 110 × 74yds
Nickname: 'Swans'	**Ground Capacity**: 16,499
Ground: Vetch Field, Swansea SA1 3SU	**Seating Capacity**: 3,414

GENERAL INFORMATION
Supporters Club Administrator:
John Button
Address: 159 Western Street, Swansea
Telephone Number: (0792) 460958
Car Parking: Kingsway Car Park (200 yards)
& Clarence Terrace Car Park (50 yards)
Coach Parking: By Police Direction
Nearest Railway Station: Swansea High
Street (0.5 mile)
Nearest Bus Station: Quadrant Depot
(0.25 mile)
Club Shop: 33 William
Street, Swansea SA1 3QS
Opening Times: Weekdays 9.30-4.30
Matchdays 9.30-5.00
Telephone No.: (0792) 462584
Postal Sales: Yes
Nearest Police Station: Swansea Central
(0.5 mile)
Police Force: South Wales
Police Telephone No.: (0792) 456999

GROUND INFORMATION
Away Supporters' Entrances: Richardson Street
Away Supporters' Sections: West Terrace Enclosure
- Partially covered

DISABLED SUPPORTERS INFORMATION
Wheelchairs: Accommodated - Centre Stand touchline
Disabled Toilets: None
The Blind: No Special Facilities

ADMISSION INFO (1993/94 PRICES)
Adult Standing: £6.00
Adult Seating: £8.50 - £9.00
Child Standing: £3.50
Child Seating: Family + 1 = £12.00 + 2 = £14.00
Programme Price: £1.00
FAX Number: (0792) 646120

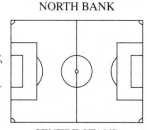

MADOC STREET
NORTH BANK

RICHARDSON STREET
WEST TERRACE (Away)

WILLIAM STREET
EAST STAND

CENTRE STAND
GLAMORGAN STREET

Travelling Supporters Information:
Routes: From All Parts: Exit M4 junction 45 and follow Swansea (A4067) signs into City Centre along High Street. Passing Railway Station into Castle Station then Wind Street and take 3rd exit at roundabout into Victoria Road and bear right towards bus station at Quadrant for Ground.

WREXHAM FC

Founded: 1873	**Record Attendance**: 34,445 (26/1/57)
Turned Professional: 1912	**Colours**: Shirts - Red
Limited Company: 1912	Shorts - White
Admitted to League: 1921	**Telephone No.**: (0978) 262129
Former Name(s): None	**Ticket Information**: (0978) 262129
Nickname: 'Robins'	**Pitch Size**: 111 × 71yds
Ground: Racecourse Ground, Mold Road,	**Ground Capacity**: 11,500
Wrexham, Clwyd	**Seating Capacity**: 5,026

GENERAL INFORMATION
Supporters Club Administrator: Miss Ena Williams
Address: c/o Club
Telephone Number: (0978) 263111
Car Parking: Town Car Parks Nearby
Coach Parking: -
Nearest Railway Station: Wrexham General (Adjacent)
Nearest Bus Station: Wrexham
Club Shop: Promotions Office
Opening Times: Matchdays Only
Telephone No.: (0978) 352536
Postal Sales: Yes
Nearest Police Station: Bodhyfryd (HQ) (1 mile)
Police Force: Wrexham Division
Police Telephone No.: (0978) 290222

GROUND INFORMATION
Away Supporters' Entrances: Mold End Turnstiles
Away Supporters' Sections: Marstons Stand, Mold End (Covered)

DISABLED SUPPORTERS INFORMATION
Wheelchairs: Accommodated in Disabled Section - Mold Road Side
Disabled Toilets: None
The Blind: Commentaries Available (Hospital Radio)

ADMISSION INFO (1993/94 PRICES)
Adult Standing: £6.00
Adult Seating: £8.00
Child Standing: £4.00
Child Seating: £6.00
Programme Price: £1.00
FAX Number: (0978) 357821

(CAR PARK)
YALE STAND

MARSTONS STAND
MOLD END
(Away)

CRISPIN LANE
KOP TOWN END

MOLD ROAD STAND

Travelling Supporters Information:
Routes: From North & West: Take A483 and Wrexham Bypass to junction with A541. Branch left and at roundabout follow Wrexham signs into Mold Road; From South & East: Take A525 or A534 into Wrexham then follow A541 signs into Mold Road.

MERTHYR TYDFIL FC

Founded: 1945
Former Name(s): Merthyr Town FC
Nickname: 'Martyrs'
Ground: Penydarren Park, Merthyr Tydfil, Mid Glamorgan
Record Attendance: 21,000 (1949)

Colours: Shirts - White/Silver/Black Squares
　　　　　Shorts - Black
Telephone No.: (0685) 371395
Daytime Phone No.: (0685) 359921
Pitch Size: 110 × 72yds
Ground Capacity: 10,000
Seating Capacity: 1,500

GENERAL INFORMATION
Supporters Club Administrator: Fred Arscott
Address: c/o Club
Telephone Number: (0685) 371395
Car Parking: Street Parking
Coach Parking: Georgetown
Nearest Railway Station: Merthyr Tydfil (0.5 mile)
Nearest Bus Station: Merthyr Tydfil
Club Shop:
Opening Times: Matchdays Only
Telephone No.: (0685) 384102
Postal Sales: Yes
Nearest Police Station: Merthyr Tydfil (0.75 mile)
Police Force: South Wales Constabulary
Police Telephone No.: (0685) 722541

GROUND INFORMATION
Away Supporters' Entrances: Theatre End
Away Supporters' Sections: Theatre End

DISABLED SUPPORTERS INFORMATION
Wheelchairs: Accommodated by Prior Arrangement
Disabled Toilets: None
The Blind: No Special Facilities

ADMISSION INFO (1993/94 PRICES)
Adult Standing: £4.00
Adult Seating: £5.00
Child Standing: £2.50
Child Seating: £3.25
Programme Price: £1.00
FAX Number: (0685) 382882
Children under 12 admitted free if with an adult.

COVERED TERRACING (AWAY)

FAMILY STAND

(PANT-MORLAIS ROAD) THEATRE END

MAIN STAND

Travelling Supporters Information:
Routes: From East: Take A465 (High Street) into Pen-y-Darren Road (about 1 mile), ground on right; From West: Take Swansea Road (A4102) past Georgetown and right into Bethesda Street, through Pant Morlais Road West into Pen-y-Darren Road. Ground on left.

CAERNARFON TOWN FC

Founded: 1876	**Contact No.**: (0286) 674045
Former Name(s): Caernarfon Athletic FC	**Pitch Size**: 111 × 74yds
Nickname: 'The Canaries'	**Ground Capacity**: 5,000
Ground: The Oval, Marcus Street, Caernarfon,	**Seating Capacity**: 330
Gwynedd	**Correspondence Address**: J.E. Watkins, c/o
Record Attendance: Not Known	20 South Penrallt, Caernarfon, Gwynedd
Colours: Shirts - Yellow	LL55 1NS
Shorts - Green	

GENERAL INFORMATION
Supporters Club Administrator: None
Address: -
Telephone Number: -
Car Parking: At Ground
Coach Parking: At Ground
Nearest Railway Station: Guide Bridge
Nearest Bus Station: Manchester
Club Shop: None
Opening Times: -
Telephone No.: -
Postal Sales: -
Nearest Police Station: William Street, Ashton-under-Lyne
Police Force: Greater Manchester
Police Telephone No.: -

Note: The photo shows 'The Oval' ground in Caernarfon but for the 1993/94 season, the club are playing in exile at Curzon Ashton's ground - National Park

DISABLED SUPPORTERS INFORMATION
Wheelchairs: Accommodated
Disabled Toilets: None
The Blind: No Special Facilities

ADMISSION INFO (1993/94 PRICES)
Adult Standing: £2.00
Adult Seating: £2.50
Child Standing: £1.50
Child Seating: £1.50
Concessionary Standing: £1.50
Concessionary Seating: £1.50
Programme Price: 60p
FAX Number: None

MAIN STAND

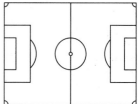

Travelling Supporters Information:
Routes: The ground is off the A635 Manchester Road in Ashton-under-Lyne, 7 miles from the City Centre behind the Ashton Police Station.

COLWYN BAY FC

Founded: 1885
Former Name(s): None
Nickname: 'Bay' or 'Seagulls'
Ground: c/o Thornton Road Stadium,
Ellesmere Port, South Wirral
Correspondence Address: 15 Smith Avenue,
Old Colwyn, Clwyd LL29 8BE

Colours: Shirts - Sky Blue
Shorts - Maroon
Telephone No.: (0492) 516941
Daytime Phone No.: (0492) 515133
Pitch Size: 110 × 75yds
Ground Capacity: 5,000
Seating Capacity: 300

GENERAL INFORMATION
Supporters Club Administrator: None
Address: -
Telephone Number: -
Car Parking: At Ground
Coach Parking: At Ground
Nearest Railway Station: Chester (10 miles)
Nearest Bus Station: Ellesmere
Club Shop: Yes at Ground
Opening Times: Matchdays only
Telephone No.: (0492) 515133 (Not Match-
days)
Postal Sales: Yes
Nearest Police Station: Ellesmere Port
Police Force: Merseyside
Police Telephone No.: -

Note : The photograph shown is that of Colwyn Bay's own ground at Llanelian Road, Old Colwyn, but for the 1993/94 Season they are ground-sharing with Ellesmere Port Town FC at their Thornton Road Stadium.

GROUND INFORMATION
Away Supporters' Entrances: No Segregation
Away Supporters' Sections: No Segregation

DISABLED SUPPORTERS INFORMATION
Wheelchairs: Accommodated
Disabled Toilets: None
The Blind: No Special Facilities

ADMISSION INFO (1993/94 PRICES)
Adult Standing: £3.00
Adult Seating: £3.00
Child Standing: £1.50
Child Seating: £1.50
Programme Price: 60p
FAX Number: None

COVERED STAND

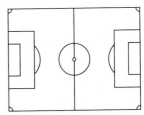

MAIN STAND

Travelling Supporters Information:
Routes: Take M56 to M53 to Ellesmere Port and exit at junction 10 onto the A5117 signposted Queensferry. Then take B5132 signposted to Ellesmere Port centre, after approximately 1 mile turn right following Thornton Road Industrial Estate and Stadium signs to Wolverham Road. Carry along across roundabout to bottom of road turn right into Thornton Road, Stadium 0.25 mile on the left.

NEWPORT AFC

Founded: 1989
Former Name(s): None
Nickname: 'The Exiles'
Ground: Somerton Park, Newport, Gwent, NP9 0HZ
Playing At: Meadow Park, Sudmeadow Road, Gloucester

Record Attendance: 2,400 vs Moreton (was 24,268 for Newport Co. vs Cardiff City 1937)
Colours: Shirts - Amber
Shorts - Amber
Contact No.: (0633) 280932
Pitch Size: 112 × 72yds
Ground Capacity: 5,000
Seating Capacity: 560

Note: The photo shows Somerton Park but for 1993/94 season, the club are playing in exile at Gloucester City's Meadow Park ground.

GENERAL INFORMATION
Supporters Club Administrator: Peter Edwards
Address: 1 Pendine Walk, Cwmbran, Gwent
Telephone Number: -
Car Parking: At Ground (150 cars)
Coach Parking: At Ground
Nearest Railway Station: Gloucester (2 mls)
Nearest Bus Station: Gloucester
Club Shop: Yes at Ground
Opening Times: Matchdays Only
Telephone No.: -
Postal Sales: c/o 66 Gibbs Road, Newport, Gwent
Nearest Police Station: Gloucester
Police Force: Gloucester Constabulary
Police Telephone No.: (0452) 521201

DISABLED SUPPORTERS INFORMATION
Wheelchairs: Accommodated by arrangement
Disabled Toilets: Yes
The Blind: No Special Facilities

ADMISSION INFO (1993/94 PRICES)
Adult Standing: £3.00
Adult Seating: £4.00
Child Standing: £2.00
Child Seating: £3.00
Concessionary Standing: £2.00 (OAP)
Concessionary Seating: £3.00 (OAP)
Programme Price: 80p
FAX Number: -

```
                MAIN STAND
 ┌──────────────────────────────────┐
 │  ┌────┐                  ┌────┐   │
O│  │    │      ( )         │    │  O│
P│  │    │       │          │    │  P│
E│  └────┘                  └────┘  E│
N│                                  N│
 │                                   │
T│  ┌────┐                  ┌────┐  T│
E│  │    │       │          │    │  E│
R│  │    │      ( )         │    │  R│
R│  └────┘                  └────┘  R│
A│                                  A│
C│                                  C│
E└──────────────────────────────────┘E
             COVERED TERRACE
```

Travelling Supporters Information:
Routes: Take A40 into Gloucester City Centre towards historic docks, then Severn Road. Turn right into Hempsted Lane and right again into Sudmeadow Road. The Ground is 50 yards on the left.

ABERYSTWYTH TOWN FC

Founded: 1884
Former Name(s): Aberystwyth FC
Nickname: 'Seasiders'
Ground: Park Avenue, Aberystwyth, Dyfed
Ground Tel. No.: (0970) 612122/617939
Pitch Size: 110 × 78yds
Record Attendance: 4,000
Ground Capacity: 2,500

Seating Capacity: 250
Correspondence Address: A.O. Griffiths,
Boars Head Hotel, Aberystwyth, Dyfed
SY23 2DH
Contact Tel. No.: (0970) 626106
FAX Number: (0970) 617939
Colours: Shirts - Green & Black
Shorts - Black

GENERAL INFORMATION
Supporters Club Administrator:
Gerwyn Richards
Address: Bryn Hyfryd, Penparcau Road,
Aberystwyth SY23 1QX
Telephone Number: -
Car Parking: Adjacent to Ground
Coach Parking: At Ground
Nearest Railway Station: Aberystwyth (0.5 mile)
Nearest Bus Station: Aberystwyth (0.5 mile)
Club Shop: Yes
Opening Times: Matchdays Only
Telephone No.: -
Postal Sales: Yes - Steve Moore c/o Club
Nearest Police Station: Aberystwyth
Police Force: Dyfed/Powys
Police Telephone No.: (0970) 612791

DISABLED SUPPORTERS INFORMATION
Wheelchairs: Accommodated - but no facilities
Disabled Toilets: None
The Blind: No Special Facilities

ADMISSION INFO (1993/94 PRICES)
Adult Standing: £2.00
Adult Seating: £2.50
Child Standing: £75p
Child Seating: £1.25
Concessionary Standing: 75p
Concessionary Seating: £1.25

OTHER INFORMATION
Programme Price: 60p
Sponsors 1993/94 Season: -

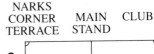

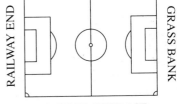

NARKS CORNER TERRACE   MAIN STAND   CLUB

RAILWAY END

GRASS BANK

COVERED TERRACE

Travelling Supporters Information:
Routes: From railway station, turn left and left again into Park Avenue, ground is at far end on right behind Bus Depot.

AFAN LIDO FC

Founded: 1967
Former Name(s): None
Nickname: -
Ground: Afan Lido Sports Ground, Aberavon, Port Talbot
Ground Tel. No.: (0639) 892960
Pitch Size: 112 × 75yds
Record Attendance: 1,100

Ground Capacity: 5,000
Seating Capacity: 125
Correspondence Address: P. Robinson, 56 Abbeyville Avenue, Sandfields Estate, Port Talbot, West Glamorgan   SA12 6PY
Contact Tel. No.: (0639) 885638
FAX Number: (0639) 885638
Colours: Shirts - Red with White Trim
Shorts - White

GENERAL INFORMATION
Supporters Club Administrator: P. Robinson
Address: 56 Abbeyville Avenue, Sandfields Estate, Port Talbot, West Glamorgan
Telephone Number: (0639) 885638
Car Parking: At Ground
Coach Parking: At Ground
Nearest Railway Station: Port Talbot Parkway
Nearest Bus Station: Port Talbot
Club Shop: At Ground
Opening Times: Matchdays Only
Telephone No.: (0639) 892960
Postal Sales: c/o Secretary
Nearest Police Station: Sandfields, Port Talbot
Police Force: South Wales Constabulary
Police Telephone No.: -

DISABLED SUPPORTERS INFORMATION
Wheelchairs: Accommodated
Disabled Toilets: Yes
The Blind: No Special Facilities

ADMISSION INFO (1993/94 PRICES)
Adult Standing: £2.00
Adult Seating: £2.50
Child Standing: Free
Child Seating: £1.00
Concessionary Standing: £1.00
Concessionary Seating: £1.50

OTHER INFORMATION
Programme Price: 50p
Sponsors 1993/94 Season: A & P Windows
Adult Season Tickets: £30.00
Child/OAP Season Tickets: £15.00

STAND

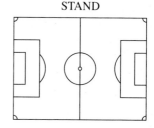

Travelling Supporters Information:
Routes: M4 to Junction 40, follow all signs to Aberavon Beach from station - past Aberavon Centre, along Water Street, Ysgythan Road and Victoria Road, right at Afan Lido.

BANGOR CITY FC

Founded: 1876
Former Name(s): Bangor Athletic FC
Nickname: 'Citizens'
Ground: The Stadium, Farrar Road, Bangor, Gwynedd
Ground Tel. No.: (0248) 355852
Pitch Size: 118 × 75yds
Record Attendance: 10,000 vs Wrexham - Welsh Cup Final 1978/79

Ground Capacity: 10,000
Seating Capacity: 900
Correspondence Address: Alun Griffiths, 12 Lon Y Bryn, Menai Bridge, Anglesey, Gwynedd LL55 5NM
Contact Tel. No.: (0248) 712820
FAX Number: (0248) 372132
Colours: Shirts - Blue
Shorts - Blue

GENERAL INFORMATION
Supporters Club Administrator: None
Address: -
Telephone Number: -
Car Parking: Street Parking & Limited space at Ground
Coach Parking: By Police Direction
Nearest Railway Station: Bangor (150 yards)
Nearest Bus Station: Bangor (500 yards)
Club Shop: Yes
Opening Times: Matchdays Only
Telephone No.: (0248) 351528
Postal Sales: c/o 30 Llys Arthur, Tan y Bryn, Bangor, Gwynedd LL57 1SP
Nearest Police Station: Bangor
Police Force: North Wales
Police Telephone No.: (0248) 370333

DISABLED SUPPORTERS INFORMATION
Wheelchairs: Accommodated
Disabled Toilets: None
The Blind: No Special Facilities

ADMISSION INFO (1993/94 PRICES)
Adult Standing: £2.00
Adult Seating: £3.00
Child Standing: £1.50
Child Seating: £2.00
Concessionary Standing: £1.50
Concessionary Seating: £2.00

OTHER INFORMATION
Programme Price: 50p
Sponsors 1993/94 Season: Pentraeth Mazda

```
                    MAIN STAND
          ┌─────────────────────────┐
   FARRER │                         │  ST. PAUL'S
   ROAD   │                         │  END
   END    │                         │
          └─────────────────────────┘
               HIGH STREET SIDE
```

Travelling Supporters Information:
Routes: Ground is on Farrar Road, 150 yards from Bangor BR Station.

BRITON FERRY ATHLETIC FC

Founded: 1926/27
Former Name(s): None
Nickname: -
Ground: Old Road, Briton Ferry, Neath, West Glamorgan
Ground Tel. No.: (0639) 812458
Pitch Size: 112 × 75yds
Record Attendance: 800 vs Abergavenny 1991/92

Ground Capacity: 2,000
Seating Capacity: 300
Correspondence Address: Graham Jenkins, 262 Neath Road, Briton Ferry SA11 2SL
Contact Tel. No.: (0639) 644755 & 814762
FAX Number: (0639) 644755
Colours: Shirts - Red & Green Quarters
　　　　Shorts - White

GENERAL INFORMATION
Supporters Club Administrator: None
Address: -
Telephone Number: -
Car Parking: Street Parking
Coach Parking: By Police Direction
Nearest Railway Station: Neath (3 miles)
Nearest Bus Station: Neath (3 miles)
Club Shop: None
Opening Times: -
Telephone No.: -
Postal Sales: -
Nearest Police Station: Briton Ferry
Police Force: South Wales Constabulary
Police Telephone No.: (0639) 812220

DISABLED SUPPORTERS INFORMATION
Wheelchairs: Accommodated
Disabled Toilets: Yes
The Blind: No Special Facilities

ADMISSION INFO (1993/94 PRICES)
Adult Standing: £2.00
Adult Seating: £3.00
Child Standing: Free
Child Seating: None
Concessionary Standing: None
Concessionary Seating: None

OTHER INFORMATION
Programme Price: 50p
Sponsors 1993/94 Season: Graham Jenkins & Son Builders

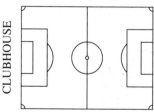

Travelling Supporters Information:
Routes: M4, then A48, right for Briton Ferry at roundabout, then right at traffic lights, ground on right. From Neath BR, right along Main Street, subway at junction, right into Briton Ferry Road, left into Cryddan Road and continue for one and a half miles past hospital, ground is on your left.

CAERSWS FC

Founded: 1887	**Seating Capacity**: 150
Former Name(s): Caersws Amateurs FC	**Correspondence Address**: T.M.B. Jones,
Nickname: 'Blue Birds'	3 Hafren Terrace, Caersws, Powys
Ground: Recreation Ground, Caersws, Powys	**Contact Tel. No.**: (0686) 688103
Ground Tel. No.: (0686) 688753	**FAX Number**: (0686) 688103
Pitch Size: 110 × 70yds	**Colours**: Shirts - Blue
Record Attendance: 2,656	Shorts - White
Ground Capacity: 3,000	

GENERAL INFORMATION
Supporters Club Administrator: None
Address: -
Telephone Number: -
Car Parking: At Ground
Coach Parking: At Ground
Nearest Railway Station: Caersws
Nearest Bus Station: Newtown
Club Shop: None
Opening Times: -
Telephone No.: -
Postal Sales: -
Nearest Police Station: Newtown
Police Force: Dyfed/Powys
Police Telephone No.: -
Village Club: (0686) 688382

DISABLED SUPPORTERS INFORMATION
Wheelchairs: Accommodated
Disabled Toilets: Yes
The Blind: No Special Facilities

ADMISSION INFO (1993/94 PRICES)
Adult Standing: £2.00
Adult Seating: £2.00
Child Standing: £1.00
Child Seating: £1.00
Concessionary Standing: £1.00
Concessionary Seating: £1.00

OTHER INFORMATION
Programme Price: 50p
Sponsors 1993/94 Season: British Beef

COVERED   COVERED
TERRACE   MAIN STAND   TERRACE

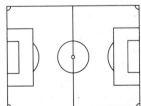

Travelling Supporters Information:
Routes: Entrance to ground at river bridge in Caersws. Caersws is situated on A470 between Newtown and Llanidloes.

CONNAH'S QUAY NOMADS FC

Founded: 1946
Former Name(s): Connah's Quay Juniors FC
Nickname: 'Westenders'
Ground: Halfway Ground, Coast Road, Connah's Quay, Deeside, Clwyd
Ground Tel. No.: (0244) 836784
Pitch Size: 110 × 70yds
Record Attendance: 1,200
Ground Capacity: 2,000

Seating Capacity: 100
Correspondence Address: R. Hunter, 40 Brookdale Avenue, Connah's Quay, Deeside, Clwyd
Contact Tel. No.: (0244) 831212
FAX Number: (0244) 836784
Colours: Shirts - White
Shorts - Black

GENERAL INFORMATION
Supporters Club Administrator: R.Edwards
Address: 29 Hadfield Close, Connah's Quay
Telephone Number: (0244) 819764
Car Parking: Street Parking
Coach Parking: At Ground
Nearest Railway Station: Shotton (1 mile)
Nearest Bus Station: Flint (2 miles)
Club Shop: None
Opening Times: -
Telephone No.: -
Postal Sales: -
Nearest Police Station: Wepre Drive, Connah's Quay
Police Force: North Wales
Police Telephone No.: (0244) 814444

DISABLED SUPPORTERS INFORMATION
Wheelchairs: Accommodated
Disabled Toilets: Yes
The Blind: No Special Facilities

ADMISSION INFO (19993/94 PRICES)
Adult Standing: £2.00
Adult Seating: £2.00
Child Standing: £1.00
Child Seating: £1.00
Concessionary Standing: £1.00
Concessionary Seating: £1.00

OTHER INFORMATION
Programme Price: 50p
Sponsors 1993/94 Season: British Steel PLC

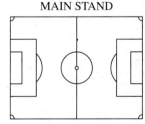

Travelling Supporters Information:
Routes: Ground is situated on the main A548 road through Connah's Quay at the rear of 'The Halfway House' pub near to the Deeside College.

CONWY UNITED FC

Founded: 1977
Former Name(s): None
Nickname: 'The Musselmen'
Ground: Morfa Ground, Conwy, Gwynedd
Ground Tel. No.: (0492) 573080
Pitch Size: 110 × 72yds
Record Attendance: 1,157
Ground Capacity: 2,000

Seating Capacity: 160
Correspondence Address: C. Jones, 'Iolyn', Iolyn Park, Conwy, Gwynedd   LL32 8UX
Contact Tel. No.: (0492) 593496
FAX Number: (0492) 623083
Colours: Shirts - Tangerine
Shorts - Black

GENERAL INFORMATION
Supporters Club Administrator: c/o Club
Address: -
Telephone Number: -
Car Parking: At Ground
Coach Parking: At Ground
Nearest Railway Station: Conwy (1 mile)
Nearest Bus Station: Llandudno Junction (1.5 miles)
Club Shop: None
Opening Times: -
Telephone No.: -
Postal Sales: Yes
Nearest Police Station: Conwy
Police Force: North Wales
Police Telephone No.: (0492) 617171

DISABLED SUPPORTERS INFORMATION
Wheelchairs: Accommodated - Railway Side
Disabled Toilets: None
The Blind: No Special Facilities

ADMISSION INFO (1993/94 PRICES)
Adult Standing: £2.00
Adult Seating: £2.50
Child Standing: £1.00 (Free if admitted with adult)
Child Seating: £1.50
Concessionary Standing: £1.00
Concessionary Seating: £1.50

OTHER INFORMATION
Programme Price: 50p
Sponsors 1993/94 Season: Crosville - Wales

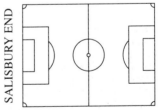

PENMORFA ROAD

SALISBURY END

CONWY END

RAILWAY SIDE STAND

Travelling Supporters Information:
Routes: From the East: Pass through A55 Expressway tunnel and take the left turn for Conwy, ground appears on left. As road passes over tunnel, continue past caravan camp, White House and Park Hall Hotels, turn left under rail bridge. From the West: On A55 Expressway take Conwy signpost after road comes round headland and link up with the above directions.

CWMBRAN TOWN FC

Founded: 1950
Former Name(s): None
Nickname: 'The Town'
Ground: Cwmbran Stadium, Henllys Way, Cwmbran, Gwent
Ground Tel. No.: (0633) 866192
Pitch Size: 112 × 76yds
Record Attendance: 3,000
Ground Capacity: 13,200

Seating Capacity: 3,200
Correspondence Address: R. Langley, 2 Trafalgar Court, Penylan Road, Penylan, Cardiff   CF2 5RL
Contact Tel. No.: (0222) 483341
FAX Number: (0633) 863324
Colours: Shirts - White - Blue Cuffs & Collars
Shorts - Red with Blue Side Stripe

GENERAL INFORMATION
Supporters Club Administrator: None
Address: -
Telephone Number: -
Car Parking: At Ground
Coach Parking: At Ground
Nearest Railway Station: Cwmbran (2 miles)
Nearest Bus Station: Cwmbran (1 mile)
Club Shop: Yes
Opening Times: Matchdays Only
Telephone No.: -
Postal Sales: Yes
Nearest Police Station: Cwmbran (1 mile)
Police Force: Gwent County
Police Telephone No.: (0633) 838999

DISABLED SUPPORTERS INFORMATION
Wheelchairs: Accommodated
Disabled Toilets: Yes
The Blind: No Special Facilities

ADMISSION INFO (1993/94 PRICES)
Adult Standing: £2.50
Adult Seating: £2.50
Child Standing: £1.25
Child Seating: £1.25
Concessionary Standing: £1.25
Concessionary Seating: £1.25

OTHER INFORMATION
Programme Price: 50p
Sponsors 1993/94 Season: B.I.G. Batteries

MAIN STAND
COVERED TERRACE

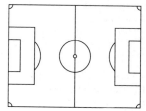

Travelling Supporters Information:
Routes: Leave M4 at junction 26. Head North on A4042. After about 3 miles turn left onto the A4051 and follow this to the 3rd roundabout. Follow sign for the stadium which is about 250 yards on the right. From the Station: On foot from the station - proceed to dual carriageway, turn left, Henllys Way is on right after one mile.

EBBW VALE FC

Founded: 1888	**Ground Capacity**: 8,000
Former Name(s): -	**Seating Capacity**: 1,000
Nickname: -	**Correspondence Address**: D. Coughlin, 107
Ground: Eugene Cross Park, Ebbw Vale,	Mount Pleasant Road, Ebbw Vale NP3 6JL
Gwent	**Contact Tel. No.**: (0495) 305993
Ground Tel. No.: (0495) 302995	**FAX Number**: -
Pitch Size: 108 × 70yds	**Colours**: Shirts - Amber
Record Attendance: Not Known	Shorts - Black

GENERAL INFORMATION
Supporters Club Administrator: None
Address: -
Telephone Number: -
Car Parking: At Ground
Coach Parking: At Ground
Nearest Railway Station: Newport
Nearest Bus Station: Newport
Club Shop: None
Opening Times: -
Telephone No.: -
Postal Sales: -
Nearest Police Station: Ebbw Vale
Police Force: Gwent
Police Telephone No.: -

DISABLED SUPPORTERS INFORMATION
Wheelchairs: Accommodated
Disabled Toilets: None
The Blind: No Special Facilities

ADMISSION INFO (1993/94 PRICES)
Adult Standing: £2.00
Adult Seating: £2.00
Child Standing: £1.00
Child Seating: £1.00
Concessionary Standing: £1.00
Concessionary Seating: £1.00

OTHER INFORMATION
Programme Price: 50p
Sponsors 1993/94 Season: -

MAIN STAND

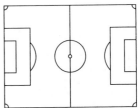

Travelling Supporters Information:
Routes: From A465 Head of Valleys Road, head for town centre, ground is by War Memorial North of the town centre.

FLINT TOWN UNITED FC

Founded: 1886	**Ground Capacity**: 3,000
Former Name(s): Flint Town FC & Flint FC	**Seating Capacity**: 215
Nickname: 'Silkmen'	**Correspondence Address**: Graham George, 49
Ground: Cae-y-Castell, Marsh Lane, Flint, Delyn, Clwyd	Third Avenue, Flint, Clwyd CH6 5LT
Ground Tel. No.: (0352) 733337	**Contact Tel. No.**: (0352) 735148
Pitch Size: 110 × 75yds	**FAX Number**: (0352) 735889
Record Attendance: Not Known	**Colours**: Shirts - Black & White Stripes
	Shorts - Black

GENERAL INFORMATION
Supporters Club Administrator: None
Address: -
Telephone Number: -
Car Parking: At Ground
Coach Parking: At Ground
Nearest Railway Station: Flint (200 yards)
Nearest Bus Station: Flint
Club Shop: Yes
Opening Times: Matchdays Only
Telephone No.: -
Postal Sales: -
Nearest Police Station: Flint
Police Force: North Wales
Police Telephone No.: (0352) 732222

Note : This is a photo of Flint Town's old ground in Holywell Road which will be in use until October 1993

DISABLED SUPPORTERS INFORMATION
Wheelchairs: Accommodated
Disabled Toilets: None
The Blind: No Special Facilities

ADMISSION INFO (1993/94 PRICES)
Adult Standing: £2.00
Adult Seating: £2.00
Child Standing: £1.00
Child Seating: £1.00
Concessionary Standing: £1.00
Concessionary Seating: £1.00

OTHER INFORMATION
Programme Price: 50p
Sponsors 1993/94 Season: Kimberley Clark

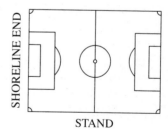

Travelling Supporters Information:
Routes: Take A458 from Connah's Quay into Flint and turn right opposite the Swan Hotel, into Castle Street following 'Castle' signs. Cross over railway and clubhouse is next to Lifeguard Station. Ground is along shoreline opposite the castle.

HAVERFORDWEST COUNTY FC

Founded: 1936
Former Name(s): None
Nickname: 'The Bluebirds'
Ground: The Bridge Meadow, Haverfordwest, Dyfed   SA61 2AL
Ground Tel. No.: (0437) 762082
Pitch Size: 110 × 70yds
Record Attendance: 5,000
Ground Capacity: 7,000

Seating Capacity: 1,100
Correspondence Address: C. Saies, 46 Wesley Place, Trecwn, Haverfordwest, Dyfed SA62 5XR
Contact Tel. No.: (0348) 840083
FAX Number: (0437) 762082
Colours: Shirts - Blue
Shorts - White

GENERAL INFORMATION
Supporters Club Administrator: -
Address: -
Telephone Number: -
Car Parking: At Ground
Coach Parking: At Ground
Nearest Railway Station: Haverfordwest
Nearest Bus Station: Haverfordwest
Club Shop: None
Opening Times: -
Telephone No.: -
Postal Sales: -
Nearest Police Station: Haverfordwest
Police Force: Dyfed/Powys
Police Telephone No.: (0437) 763355

DISABLED SUPPORTERS INFORMATION
Wheelchairs: Accommodated
Disabled Toilets: None
The Blind: No Special Facilities

ADMISSION INFO (1993/94 PRICES)
Adult Standing: £2.00
Adult Seating: £2.00
Child Standing: £1.00
Child Seating: £1.00
Concessionary Standing: £1.00
Concessionary Seating: £1.00

OTHER INFORMATION
Programme Price: 50p
Sponsors 1993/94 Season: Various

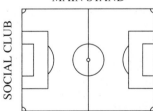

Travelling Supporters Information:
Routes: A40 to Haverfordwest, ground adjacent to main road on North side of town centre. From station, left, follow ring road past town centre. Enter ground via subway.

HOLYWELL TOWN FC

Founded: 1948	**Ground Capacity**: 4,000
Former Name(s): None	**Seating Capacity**: 500
Nickname: 'The Wellmen'	**Correspondence Address**: Glyn M. Davies, 45
Ground: Halkyn Road Ground, Halkyn Street,	Bron-Y-Wern, Bagilli, Clwyd CH6 6BS
Holywell, Clwyd	**Contact Tel. No.**: (0352) 763571
Ground Tel. No.: (0352) 711411	**FAX Number**: (0352) 711411
Pitch Size: 115 × 72yds	**Colours**: Shirts - Red & White Stripes
Record Attendance: 3,000	Shorts - Blue

GENERAL INFORMATION
Supporters Club Administrator: None
Address: -
Telephone Number: -
Car Parking: At Ground
Coach Parking: At Ground
Nearest Railway Station: Flint (4 miles)
Nearest Bus Station: Holywell (0.5 mile)
Club Shop: Yes
Opening Times: Matchdays Only
Telephone No.: (0352) 711411
Postal Sales: -
Nearest Police Station: Holywell
Police Force: Clwyd
Police Telephone No.: (0352) 711669

DISABLED SUPPORTERS INFORMATION
Wheelchairs: Accommodated
Disabled Toilets: None
The Blind: No Special Facilities

ADMISSION INFO (1993/94 PRICES)
Adult Standing: £2.00
Adult Seating: £2.00
Child Standing: £1.00
Child Seating: £1.00
Concessionary Standing: 50p
Concessionary Seating: 50p

OTHER INFORMATION
Programme Price: 50p
Sponsors 1993/94 Season: Rank Xerox

HALKYN ROAD HEALTH CENTRE

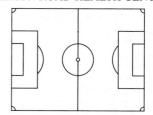

Travelling Supporters Information:
Routes: From town centre, proceed down Halkyn Road past Police Station & ground is on the left down an approach road (clearly signposted) at the rear of the Health Centre.

INTER CARDIFF FC

Founded: 1990
Former Name(s): Sully FC
Nickname: 'Seagulls'
Ground: Ninian Park, Sloper Road, Cardiff CF1 8SX
Ground Tel. No.: (0222) 398636
Pitch Size: 112 × 76yds
Record Attendance: 61,566
(Cardiff City 14/10/61)

Ground Capacity: 21,403
Seating Capacity: 12,500
Correspondence Address: Ninian Park, Sloper Road, Cardiff
Contact Tel. No.: (0222) 398636
Colours: Shirts - White & Black
Shorts - Red Socks

GENERAL INFORMATION
Supporters Club Administrator: Peter Woollacott
Address: c/o Ninian Park, Sloper Road
Car Parking: Sloper Road
Coach Parking: Sloper Road
Nearest Railway Station: Cardiff Central (1 mile)
Nearest Bus Station: Cardiff Central
Club Shop: None
Opening Times: -
Telephone No.: -
Postal Sales: -
Nearest Police Station: Cowbridge Road Estate, Cardiff
Police Force: South Wales
Police Telephone No.: (0222) 222111

DISABLED SUPPORTERS INFORMATION
Wheelchairs: Accommodated Canton Stand
Disabled Toilets: None
The Blind: No Special Facilities

ADMISSION INFO (1993/94 PRICES)
Male Adult Standing: £2.00
Male Adult Seating: £2.00
Women/Child Standing: Free
Women/Child Seating: Free
Concessionary Standing: -
Concessionary Seating: -

OTHER INFORMATION
Programme Price: 50p
Sponsors 1993/94 Season: S.A. Brain

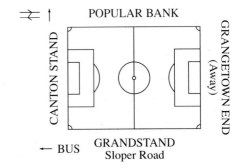

Travelling Supporters Information:
Routes: From North: Take A470 until Junction with Cardiff Bypass. Then 3rd exit at Roundabout A48 to Port Talbot, after 2 miles take 1st exit at Roundabout A4161 (Cowbridge Road). Turn right (0.5 mile), Lansdowne Road to Crossroads, turn right into Leckwith Road, then turn left (0.25 mile) into Sloper Road. From East: Exit M4 taking A48 to Cardiff Bypass (then as North). From West: Take A4161 Cowbridge Road (then as North).
Bus Services: Service No.2 - City Centre to Ground and Service No.1

LLANELLI AFC

Founded: 1896
Former Name(s): None
Nickname: 'Reds'
Ground: Stebonheath Park, Llanelli, Dyfed
Ground Tel. No.: (0554) 772973
Pitch Size: 114 × 73yds
Record Attendance: 18,000 vs Bristol Rovers
Ground Capacity: 3,700

Seating Capacity: 700
Correspondence Address: R. Davies, 29 Pemberton Park, Llanelli, Dyfed SA14 8NN
Contact Tel. No.: (0554) 756176
FAX Number: (0544) 751958
Colours: Shirts - Red
Shorts - Red

GENERAL INFORMATION
Supporters Club Administrator: -
Address: -
Telephone Number: -
Car Parking: At Ground
Coach Parking: At Ground
Nearest Railway Station: Llanelli (2 miles)
Nearest Bus Station: Llanelli (1 mile)
Club Shop: None
Opening Times: -
Telephone No.: -
Postal Sales: -
Nearest Police Station: Llanelli (1 mile)
Police Force: Dyfed/Powys
Police Telephone No.: (0554) 772222

DISABLED SUPPORTERS INFORMATION
Wheelchairs: Accommodated
Disabled Toilets: Yes - in clubhouse
The Blind: No Special Facilities

ADMISSION INFO (1993/94 PRICES)
Adult Standing: £2.00
Adult Seating: £2.00
Child Standing: £1.00
Child Seating: £1.00
Concessionary Standing: £1.00
Concessionary Seating: £1.00

OTHER INFORMATION
Programme Price: 50p
Sponsors 1993/94 Season: -

CLUBHOUSE

TERRACING

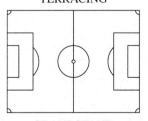

GRANDSTAND

Travelling Supporters Information:
Routes: M4 to junction 48, A4138, right at lights then left into Penallt Road. From station - Station Road to centre, right along Murray Street, Stepney Place, James Street, right into Alban Road then left into Bedford Street and right into Evans Terrace.

Llansantffraid FC

Founded: 1959	**Seating Capacity**: 130
Former Name(s): None	**Correspondence Address**: G.M.G. Ellis,
Nickname: 'Saints'	Brodawel, Church Lane, Llansantffraid, Powys
Ground: Recreation Ground, Treflan, Llansant-ffraid, Powys	SY22 6AP
Ground Tel. No.: (0691) 828112	**Contact Tel. No.**: (0691) 828583
Pitch Size: 110 × 75yds	**FAX Number**: (0691) 828112
Record Attendance: 500	**Colours**: Shirts - Green
Ground Capacity: 1,500	Shorts - Black

GENERAL INFORMATION
Supporters Club Administrator: None
Address: -
Telephone Number: -
Car Parking: At Ground
Coach Parking: At Ground
Nearest Railway Station: Gobowen & Welshpool
Nearest Bus Station: Oswestry
Club Shop: At Clubhouse
Opening Times: During Opening Times
Telephone No.: (0691) 828112
Postal Sales: Brodawel, Llansantffraid
Nearest Police Station: Llanfyllin
Police Force: Dyfed/Powys
Police Telephone No.: (0691) 648222

DISABLED SUPPORTERS INFORMATION
Wheelchairs: Accommodated
Disabled Toilets: Yes
The Blind: No Special Facilities

ADMISSION INFO (1993/94 PRICES)
Adult Standing: £2.00
Adult Seating: £2.00
Child Standing: 50p
Child Seating: 50p
Concessionary Standing: -
Concessionary Seating: -

OTHER INFORMATION
Programme Price: 50p
Sponsors 1993/94 Season: Mike Hughes & J.T. Hughes

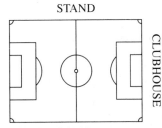

STAND

CLUBHOUSE

CHANGING ROOMS

Travelling Supporters Information:
Routes: Take the B4393 off the A483 Welshpool to Oswestry Road at 'Four Crosses' and head into Llansantffraid. The ground is in the centre of the village opposite Wynnstay Farmers Mill.

MAESTEG PARK FC

Founded: 1945
Former Name(s): Maesteg Park Athletic FC
Nickname: 'The Park'
Ground: Tudor Park, St. David's Place, Park Estate, Maesteg, Mid Glam.
Ground Tel. No.: (0656) 732092
Pitch Size: 112 × 78yds
Record Attendance: 1,000
Ground Capacity: 2,000

Seating Capacity: 200
Correspondence Address: D. Griffiths, 3 Padley's Close, Maesteg, Bridgend, Mid Glam. CF34 0TX
Contact Tel. No.: (0656) 733000
FAX Number: (0656) 732519
Colours: Shirts - Blue with White Trim
　　　　　Shorts - Blue

GENERAL INFORMATION
Supporters Club Administrator: None
Address: c/o Clubhouse (at Ground)
Telephone Number: (0656) 732029
Car Parking: At Ground
Coach Parking: At Ground
Nearest Railway Station: Maesteg
Nearest Bus Station: Maesteg
Club Shop: Yes
Opening Times: Matchdays Only
Telephone No.: (0656) 732092
Postal Sales: -
Nearest Police Station: Maesteg
Police Force: Mid Glamorgan
Police Telephone No.: (0656) 732122

DISABLED SUPPORTERS INFORMATION
Wheelchairs: Accommodated
Disabled Toilets: None
The Blind: No Special Facilities

ADMISSION INFO (1993/94 PRICES)
Adult Standing: £2.00
Adult Seating: £2.00
Child Standing: £1.00
Child Seating: £1.00
Concessionary Standing: £1.00
Concessionary Seating: £1.00

OTHER INFORMATION
Programme Price: 50p
Sponsors 1993/94 Season: -

Travelling Supporters Information:
Routes: Leave M4 at junction 36, A4063 to Cross Inn at Cwmfelin, turn left into R.H. lane up steep hill, ground on top on left after passing Red Cow pub on right. On foot - take West Street from town centre (turning off Commercial Street), up hill then left at junction. Ground is on your right.

MOLD ALEXANDRA FC

Founded: 1929
Former Name(s): -
Nickname: -
Ground: Alyn Parc, Mold, Clwyd
Ground Tel. No.: (0352) 4007
Pitch Size: 108 × 72yds
Record Attendance: Not Known
Ground Capacity: 2,000

Seating Capacity: 50
Correspondence Address: D. Williams, 45 Dreflan Road, Mold, Clwyd
Contact Tel. No.: -
FAX Number: -
Colours: Shirts - Blue & Red
Shorts - Blue & Red

GENERAL INFORMATION
Supporters Club Administrator: None
Address: -
Telephone Number: -
Car Parking: At Ground
Coach Parking: At Ground
Nearest Railway Station: Wrexham/Flint
Nearest Bus Station: Wrexham
Club Shop: None
Opening Times: -
Telephone No.: -
Postal Sales: -
Nearest Police Station: Mold
Police Force: North Wales
Police Telephone No.: -

DISABLED SUPPORTERS INFORMATION
Wheelchairs: Accommodated
Disabled Toilets: None
The Blind: No Special Facilities

ADMISSION INFO (1993/94 PRICES)
Adult Standing: £2.00
Adult Seating: £2.00
Child Standing: £1.00
Child Seating: £1.00
Concessionary Standing: £1.00
Concessionary Seating: £1.00

OTHER INFORMATION
Programme Price: 50p
Sponsors 1993/94 Season: -

Travelling Supporters Information:
Routes: Ground is on Denbigh Road. From town centre follow signs for Denbigh, approach road is on right hand side of Denbigh Road, 100 yards before Blue Bell Pub.

NEWTOWN AFC

Founded: 1875
Former Name(s): Newtown Whitestars FC
Nickname: 'The Robins'
Ground: Latham Park, Newtown, Powys
Ground Tel. No.: (0686) 626159
Pitch Size: 112 × 72yds
Record Attendance: 5,004
Ground Capacity: 5,000

Seating Capacity: 220
Correspondence Address: K. Harding, 7
Tradyddan Terrace, Newtown, Powys
SY16 2ER
Contact Tel. No.: (0686) 628523
FAX Number: (0686) 623813
Colours: Shirts - Red
Shorts - White

GENERAL INFORMATION
Supporters Club Administrator: -
Address: c/o Club
Telephone Number: 90686) 626159
Car Parking: At Ground
Coach Parking: At Ground
Nearest Railway Station: Newtown
Nearest Bus Station: Newtown Back Lane
Club Shop: Yes
Opening Times: Matchdays Only
Telephone No.: (0686) 626159
Postal Sales: Yes
Nearest Police Station: Newtown
Police Force: Dyfed/Powys
Police Telephone No.: (0686) 622777

DISABLED SUPPORTERS INFORMATION
Wheelchairs: Accommodated
Disabled Toilets: None
The Blind: No Special Facilities

ADMISSION INFO (1993/94 PRICES)
Adult Standing: £2.00
Adult Seating: £2.00
Child Standing: 50p
Child Seating: 50p
Concessionary Standing: 50p
Concessionary Seating: 50p

OTHER INFORMATION
Programme Price: 50p
Sponsors 1993/94 Season: -

```
        SOCIAL
        CLUB    STAND

P                           R
A                           I
V                           V
I                           E
L                           R
I                           
O                           E
N                           N
                            D
E
N
D

        TOWN SIDE TERRACING
```

Travelling Supporters Information:
Routes: On fringe of town centre, behind Police Station. Turn into Park Lane from Park Street by Town Library. Ground is 800 yards along Park Lane.

PORTHMADOG FC

Founded: 1884
Former Name(s): None
Nickname: 'Port'
Ground: Y Traeth, Porthmadog, Gwynedd
Ground Tel. No.: (0766) 514687
Pitch Size: 116 × 76yds
Record Attendance: 3,500
Ground Capacity: 4,000

Seating Capacity: 250
Correspondence Address: R.I. Griffiths, Llw-yn-yr-Eryr, Ynys, Criccieth   LL52 0PB
Contact Tel. No.: (0766) 810349
FAX Number: (0766) 514687
Colours: Shirts - Red & Black Stripes
Shorts - White

GENERAL INFORMATION
Supporters Club Administrator: -
Address: c/o Club
Telephone Number: -
Car Parking: At Ground
Coach Parking: At Ground
Nearest Railway Station: Porthmadog
Nearest Bus Station: Porthmadog
Club Shop: None
Opening Times: -
Telephone No.: -
Postal Sales: -
Nearest Police Station: Porthmadog
Police Force: North Wales
Police Telephone No.: (0766) 512226

DISABLED SUPPORTERS INFORMATION
Wheelchairs: Accommodated
Disabled Toilets: None
The Blind: No Special Facilities

ADMISSION INFO (1993/94 PRICES)
Adult Standing: £2.00
Adult Seating: £3.00
Child Standing: £1.00
Child Seating: £2.00
Concessionary Standing: -
Concessionary Seating: -

OTHER INFORMATION
Programme Price: 50p
Sponsors 1993/94 Season: Bourne Leisure Group

CAR PARK
TOWN END
QUARRY END
MAIN STAND
PIKE'S SHELTER

Travelling Supporters Information:
Routes: At crossroads in town (by Woolworths), go down Snowdon Street, cross over Madog Street and walk past British Legion Club and Porthmadog Pottery Workshop, carry on over railway crossing, ground is on your right. (Total distance 1 mile). Alternatively turn at the side of British Rail and West Highland Railway Stations into Cambrian terrace and continue for half a mile then turn at fish and chip shop past Porthmadog Pottery (then as above).

TON PENTRE FC

Founded: 1935	**Ground Capacity**: 2,700
Former Name(s): None	**Seating Capacity**: 530
Nickname: 'Bulldogs'	**Correspondence Address**: P. Willoughby, 37
Ground: Ynys Park, Ton Row, Ton Pentre,	Bailey Street, Ton Pentre, Rhondda CF41 7EN
Rhondda	**Contact Tel. No.**: (0443) 438281
Ground Tel. No.: (0443) 432813	**FAX Number**: -
Pitch Size: 110 × 70yds	**Colours**: Shirts - Red
Record Attendance: 6,000 vs Falmouth	Shorts - Red

GENERAL INFORMATION
Supporters Club Administrator: None
Address: -
Telephone Number: -
Car Parking: At Ground
Coach Parking: Llanfoist Street
Nearest Railway Station: Ton Pentre
Nearest Bus Station: Ton Pentre
Club Shop: None
Opening Times: -
Telephone No.: -
Postal Sales: -
Nearest Police Station: Ton Pentre
Police Force: South Wales
Police Telephone No.: -

DISABLED SUPPORTERS INFORMATION
Wheelchairs: Accommodated
Disabled Toilets: None
The Blind: No Special Facilities

ADMISSION INFO (1993/94 PRICES)
Adult Standing: £2.00
Adult Seating: £2.00
Child Standing: £1.00
Child Seating: £1.00
Concessionary Standing: £1.00
Concessionary Seating: £1.00

OTHER INFORMATION
Programme Price: 50p
Sponsors 1993/94 Season: -

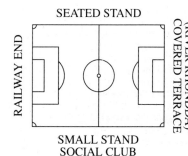

Travelling Supporters Information:
Routes: Exit M4 junction 34, and follow signs for Rhondda Valley & Treorchy. On reaching Pentre turn left over rail bridge then 1st left again for club.

BRYMBO FC

Founded: 1943
Former Name(s): Brymbo Steelworks FC
Nickname: -
Ground: Brymbo Steelworks Sports Complex,
Tanyfron, Wrexham
Ground Tel. No.: (0978) 755886
Pitch Size: 108 × 72yds
Record Attendance: Not Known
Ground Capacity: 800

Seating Capacity: -
Correspondence Address: N. Jones, 29 Bryn-
Coed, Gwersyllt, Wrexham, Clwyd
LL11 4UE
Contact Tel. No.: (0978) 753250
FAX Number: -
Colours: Shirts - Yellow
          Shorts - Black

GENERAL INFORMATION
Supporters Club Administrator: None
Address: -
Telephone Number: -
Car Parking: At Ground
Coach Parking: At Ground
Nearest Railway Station: Wrexham
Nearest Bus Station: Wrexham
Club Shop: None
Opening Times: -
Telephone No.: -
Postal Sales: -
Nearest Police Station: Wrexham
Police Force: North Wales
Police Telephone No.: (0978) 290222

DISABLED SUPPORTERS INFORMATION
Wheelchairs: Accommodated
Disabled Toilets: None
The Blind: No Special Facilities

ADMISSION INFO (1993/94 PRICES)
Adult Standing: £1.00
Child Standing: 50p
Concessionary Standing: 50p

OTHER INFORMATION
Programme Price: 50p
Sponsors 1993/94 Season: -

COVERED STANDING

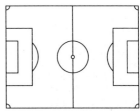

COVERED STANDING

Travelling Supporters Information:
Routes: The Ground is situated within the Brymbo Steelworks Sports Complex at Tanyfron, Wrexham.

CARNO FC

Founded: 1960
Former Name(s): -
Nickname: -
Ground: Recreation Ground, Carno, Powys
Ground Tel. No.: -
Pitch Size: 110 × 72yds
Record Attendance: Not Known
Ground Capacity: 3,000

Seating Capacity: 100
Correspondence Address: Mrs T. Hughes, 32 Maes y Dre, Caersws, Powys
Contact Tel. No.: (0686) 688713
FAX Number: -
Colours: Shirts - Green
Shorts - Black

GENERAL INFORMATION
Supporters Club Administrator: None
Address: -
Telephone Number: -
Car Parking: At Ground
Coach Parking: At Ground
Nearest Railway Station: Caersws
Nearest Bus Station: Newtown
Club Shop: None
Opening Times: -
Telephone No.: -
Postal Sales: -
Nearest Police Station: Newtown
Police Force: Dyfed/Powys
Police Telephone No.: (0686) 622777

DISABLED SUPPORTERS INFORMATION
Wheelchairs: Accommodated
Disabled Toilets: None
The Blind: No Special Facilities

ADMISSION INFO (1993/94 PRICES)
Adult Standing: £1.00
Adult Seating: £1.00
Child Standing: 50p
Child Seating: 50p
Concessionary Standing: 50p
Concessionary Seating: 50p

OTHER INFORMATION
Programme Price: 50p
Sponsors 1993/94 Season: -

MAIN STAND

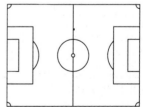

Travelling Supporters Information:
Routes: Ground is situated at the recreation ground in Carno, Powys.

CEFN DRUIDS FC

Founded: 1992 (amalgamation of Cefn Albion FC & Druids United FC)	**Ground Capacity**: 2,000
	Seating Capacity: None
Former Name(s): Cefn Albion FC, Druids United FC	**Correspondence Address**: S. Williams, 9 Beacon Road, Pendine Park, Summerhill, Wrexham LL11 4UW
Nickname: 'Zebras'	
Ground: Plaskynaston, Cefn Mawr, Wrexham, Clwyd	**Contact Tel. No.**: (0978) 752489
	FAX Number: None
Pitch Size: 110 × 72yds	**Colours**: Shirts - White
Record Attendance: Not Known	Shorts - Black

GENERAL INFORMATION
Supporters Club Administrator: G. Wiblin
Address: c/o Kronospan Ltd., Chirk, Clwyd
Telephone Number: (0691) 775254 (Days)
Car Parking: At Ground
Coach Parking: At Ground
Nearest Railway Station: Ruabon
Nearest Bus Station: Wrexham
Club Shop: None
Opening Times: -
Telephone No.: -
Postal Sales: Yes
Nearest Police Station: Ruabon
Police Force: Wrexham Division
Police Telephone No.: (0978) 290222

DISABLED SUPPORTERS INFORMATION
Wheelchairs: Not Accommodated
Disabled Toilets: None
The Blind: No Special Facilities

ADMISSION INFO (1993/94 PRICES)
Adult Standing: £1.00
Child Standing: 50p
Concessionary Standing: None

OTHER INFORMATION
Programme Price: 50p
Sponsors 1993/94 Season: David Jackson Insurance

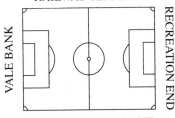

Travelling Supporters Information:
Routes: From the North & West: Take the A483 and Wrexham Bypass to junction with A539 then turn left on the B5605 then right on the B5096. Turn left at Kwik Save supermarket down a narrow lane to the Ground and Car Park. From the South & East: Take the A525 then turn left on the A528 then right on the A539 then as North & West route from the B5605 to the Ground.

CEMAES BAY FC

Founded: 1976	**Seating Capacity**: 150
Former Name(s): None	**Correspondence Address**: Mrs. Nell Hughes,
Nickname: 'Demolition Squad'	12 Maes Garnedd, Tregele
Ground: School Lane Stadium, Cemaes Bay,	**Contact Tel. No.**: (0407) 710297
Anglesey, Gwynedd	**FAX Number**: None
Pitch Size: 110 × 72yds	**Colours**: Shirts - Red
Record Attendance: 1,600	Shorts - Red
Ground Capacity: 4,000	

GENERAL INFORMATION
Supporters Club Administrator: None
Address: -
Telephone Number: -
Car Parking: At Ground
Coach Parking: In Roadway - Adjacent
Nearest Railway Station: River (10 miles)
Nearest Bus Station: Bangor (40 miles)
Club Shop: None
Opening Times: -
Telephone No.: -
Postal Sales: -
Nearest Police Station: Cemaes Bay
Police Force: North Wales
Police Telephone No.: (0407) 710222

DISABLED SUPPORTERS INFORMATION
Wheelchairs: Not Accommodated
Disabled Toilets: None
The Blind: No Special Facilities

ADMISSION INFO (1993/94 PRICES)
Adult Standing: £2.00
Adult Seating: £2.00
Child Standing: £1.00
Child Seating: £1.00
Concessionary Standing: £1.00
Concessionary Seating: £1.00

OTHER INFORMATION
Programme Price: 50p
Sponsors 1993/94 Season: George Fletcher Demolition

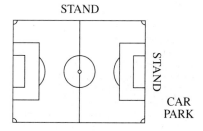

Travelling Supporters Information:
Routes: Take the A5 towards Holyhead and turn right at the 'Valley' crossroads (a little before Holyhead) onto the A5025. After about 9 miles, pass the turn-off for the Wylfa Nuclear Power Station and continue to the roundabout in Cemaes. Turn right at roundabout for Llanfechell and after 100 yards turn left opposite Police House. Ground is down the track between houses.

GRESFORD ATHLETIC FC

Founded: 1946
Former Name(s): None
Nickname: 'Athletic'
Ground: Clappers Lane, Chester Road, Gresford, Wrexham, Clwyd
Ground Tel. No.: None
Pitch Size: 110 × 75yds
Record Attendance: Not Known
Ground Capacity: 1,000

Seating Capacity: None at Present
Correspondence Address: D.C. Rowland, 26 Gorse Crescent, Marford, Wrexham, Clwyd LL12 8QZ
Contact Tel. No.: (0978) 855354
FAX Number: None
Colours: Shirts - Red
Shorts - White

GENERAL INFORMATION
Supporters Club Administrator: None
Address: -
Telephone Number: -
Car Parking: At Ground
Coach Parking: At Ground
Nearest Railway Station: Wrexham
Nearest Bus Station: Wrexham
Club Shop: None
Opening Times: -
Telephone No.: -
Postal Sales: -
Nearest Police Station: Gresford
Police Force: Wrexham Division
Police Telephone No.: (0978) 290222

DISABLED SUPPORTERS INFORMATION
Wheelchairs: Accommodated
Disabled Toilets: None
The Blind: No Special Facilities

ADMISSION INFO (1993/94 PRICES)
Adult Standing: £1.00
Child Standing: 50p
Concessionary Standing: None

OTHER INFORMATION
Programme Price: 50p
Sponsors 1993/94 Season: P & J Cars

Travelling Supporters Information:
Routes: Ground is on the main Chester to Wrexham Road (not the bypass), approximately 4 miles from Wrexham next to the Texaco Garage.

KNIGHTON TOWN FC

Founded: 1881	**Seating Capacity**: 50
Former Name(s): -	**Correspondence Address**: Mrs. C.A. Sutton,
Nickname: 'Town'	"Ashdown", 1 Underhill Crescent, Knighton,
Ground: Bryn Y Castell, Knighton, Powys	Powys LD7 1DG
Ground Tel. No.: (0547) 528999	**Contact Tel. No.**: (0547) 528953
Pitch Size: 110 × 72yds	**FAX Number**: None
Record Attendance: Not Known	**Colours**: Shirts - Red
Ground Capacity: 2,000	Shorts - White

GENERAL INFORMATION
Supporters Club Administrator: None
Address: -
Telephone Number: -
Car Parking: At Ground
Coach Parking: At Ground
Nearest Railway Station: Knighton
Nearest Bus Station: Knighton
Club Shop: None
Opening Times: -
Telephone No.: -
Postal Sales: -
Nearest Police Station: Knighton
Police Force: Dyfed/Powys
Police Telephone No.: -

DISABLED SUPPORTERS INFORMATION
Wheelchairs: Accommodated
Disabled Toilets: None
The Blind: No Special Facilities

ADMISSION INFO (1993/94 PRICES)
Adult Standing: £1.00
Adult Seating: £1.00
Child Standing: 50p
Child Seating: 50p
Concessionary Standing: 50p
Concessionary Seating: 50p

OTHER INFORMATION
Programme Price: -
Sponsors 1993/94 Season: -

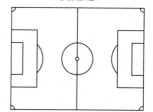
CLUBHOUSE
STAND

Travelling Supporters Information:
Routes: Ground is situated on A4113 South East of Town Centre.

LEX XI FC

Founded: 1965	**Ground Capacity**: 500
Former Name(s): Stansty Park FC	**Seating Capacity**: None
Nickname: -	**Correspondence Address**: P.L. Jones, 18 May-
Ground: Stansty Park, Mold Road, Wrexham,	flower Drive, Marford, Wrexham LL12 8LD
Clwyd	**Contact Tel. No.**: (0978) 854028
Ground Tel. No.: (0978) 262129	**FAX Number**: None
Pitch Size: 108 × 74yds	**Colours**: Shirts - Amber
Record Attendance: Not Known	Shorts - Black

GENERAL INFORMATION
Supporters Club Administrator: None
Address: -
Telephone Number: -
Car Parking: -
Coach Parking: At Ground
Nearest Railway Station: Wrexham General
Nearest Bus Station: King Street, Wrexham
(1 mile)
Club Shop: None
Opening Times: -
Telephone No.: -
Postal Sales: -
Nearest Police Station: Wrexham
Police Force: Wrexham Division
Police Telephone No.: (0978) 290222

DISABLED SUPPORTERS INFORMATION
Wheelchairs: Not Accommodated
Disabled Toilets: None
The Blind: No Special Facilities

ADMISSION INFO (1993/94 PRICES)
Adult Standing: £1.00
Child Standing: 50p
Concessionary Standing: 50p

OTHER INFORMATION
Programme Price: 50p
Sponsors 1993/94 Season: Dave Bennett - Accident
Repairs

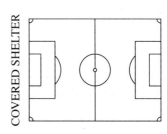

Travelling Supporters Information:
Routes: The ground is situated on a triangular piece of pland known as Stansty Park inbetween Summerhill
Road and Mold Road on the outskirts of Wrexham. 2 miles from Town Centre and one mile from Wrexham
FC's Racecourse Ground.

LLANDUDNO TOWN FC

Founded: 1966	**Ground Capacity**: 6,000
Former Name(s): Llandudno Amateurs	**Seating Capacity**: None
Nickname: 'Town'	**Correspondence Address**: B. Jarvis, 10
Ground: Maesdu Park, Builder Street,	Howard Road, Llandudno LL30 1EA
Llandudno, Gwynedd	**Contact Tel. No.**: (0492) 877113
Ground Tel. No.: None	**FAX Number**: None
Pitch Size: 110 × 70yds	**Colours**: Shirts - White
Record Attendance: Not Known	Shorts - Navy Blue

GENERAL INFORMATION
Supporters Club Administrator: None
Address: -
Telephone Number: ?
Car Parking: At Ground
Coach Parking: At Ground
Nearest Railway Station: Llandudno (0.5ml)
Nearest Bus Station: Llandudno Junction
Club Shop: None
Opening Times: -
Telephone No.: -
Postal Sales: -
Nearest Police Station: Llandudno
Police Force: North Wales
Police Telephone No.: -

DISABLED SUPPORTERS INFORMATION
Wheelchairs: Accommodated
Disabled Toilets: None
The Blind: No Special Facilities

ADMISSION INFO (1993-94 PRICES)
Adult Standing: £2.00
Child Standing: £1.00
Concessionary Standing: £1.00

OTHER INFORMATION
Programme Price: 50p
Sponsors 1993/94 Season: -

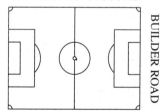

COVERED ENCLOSURE

BUILDER ROAD

TURNSTILES
COACH PARK

Travelling Supporters Information:
Routes: Take the A55 Expressway to the Llandudno Junction exit (next to Conwy Tunnel) and take 2nd exit at roundabout for Deganwy (A546). Pass through Deganwy and head into Llandudno. After Golf Course take right hand turn before railway bridge then 1st right into Builder Street West. Ground is on right next to the coach park.

LLANIDLOES TOWN FC

Founded: 1875
Former Name(s): Llanidloes United FC
Nickname: 'The Daffs'
Ground: Victoria Avenue, Llanidloes, Powys
Ground Tel. No.: (0686) 412550
Pitch Size: 112 × 72yds
Record Attendance: 3,000 vs Swansea (1971)
Ground Capacity: 3,500

Seating Capacity: 200
Correspondence Address: G.E. Parry, 22 Llysnant, Llanidloes, Powys SY18 6BD
Contact Tel. No.: (0686) 412550
FAX Number: -
Colours: Shirts - Yellow
       Shorts - Green

GENERAL INFORMATION
Supporters Club Administrator: I. Jerman
Address: c/o Club
Telephone Number: (0686) 412196
Car Parking: At Ground
Coach Parking: At Ground
Nearest Railway Station: Caersws
Nearest Bus Station: Llanidloes
Club Shop: None
Opening Times: -
Telephone No.: -
Postal Sales: -
Nearest Police Station: Llanidloes
Police Force: Dyfed/Powys
Police Telephone No.: (0551) 222222

DISABLED SUPPORTERS INFORMATION
Wheelchairs: Accommodated
Disabled Toilets: None
The Blind: No Special Facilities

ADMISSION INFO (1993/94 PRICES)
Adult Standing: £2.00
Adult Seating: £2.00
Child Standing: £1.00
Child Seating: £1.00
Concessionary Standing: £1.00
Concessionary Seating: £1.00

OTHER INFORMATION
Programme Price: 50p
Sponsors 1993/94 Season: -

STAND

DRILL HALL END

FOUNDRY END

MAIN STAND
VICTORIA AVENUE

Travelling Supporters Information:
Routes: Victoria Park is situated alongside the B4518 half a mile from its Northern Junction with the A470 Trunk Road (Llanidloes By-Pass). If approaching from South Wales take second exit from by-pass.

MOSTYN FC

Founded: 1912	**Seating Capacity**: None
Former Name(s): -	**Correspondence Address**: B. Hughes, 11
Nickname: None	Penrho Estate, Mostyn, Clwyd
Ground: Maes Pennant, Mostyn, Clwyd	**Contact Tel. No.**: (0745) 560822
Ground Tel. No.: None	**FAX Number**: None
Pitch Size: 108 × 70yds	**Colours**: Shirts - Yellow
Record Attendance: Not Known	Shorts - Blue
Ground Capacity: 800	

GENERAL INFORMATION
Supporters Club Administrator: None
Address: -
Telephone Number: -
Car Parking: Street Parking
Coach Parking: Street Parking
Nearest Railway Station: Prestatyn (4 miles)
Nearest Bus Station: Prestatyn (4 miles)
Club Shop: None
Opening Times: -
Telephone No.: -
Postal Sales: -
Nearest Police Station: Prestatyn
Police Force: North Wales
Police Telephone No.: -

DISABLED SUPPORTERS INFORMATION
Wheelchairs: Not Accommodated
Disabled Toilets: None
The Blind: No Special Facilities

ADMISSION INFO (1993/94 PRICES)
Adult Standing: £1.00
Child Standing: 50p
Concessionary Standing: None

OTHER INFORMATION
Programme Price: £1.00 (includes admission)
Sponsors 1993/94 Season: -

SHELTER

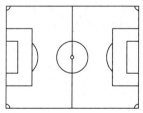

Travelling Supporters Information:
Routes: On reaching Mostyn village, ground is opposite the shops, 100 yards walk on the left.
NOTE : Village is situated uphill from the A548.

PENLEY FC

Founded: 1972	**Ground Capacity**: Open Area
Former Name(s): None	**Seating Capacity**: None
Nickname: -	**Correspondence Address**: A.Peate, Old Police
Ground: The Maelor School, Penley,	House, Hanmer, Nr. Whitchurch SY13 3DE
Nr. Wrexham, Clwyd	**Contact Tel. No.**: (094) 874517
Ground Tel. No.: None	**FAX Number**: None
Pitch Size: 110 × 70yds	**Colours**: Shirts - Yellow
Record Attendance: 200	Shorts - Blue

GENERAL INFORMATION
Supporters Club Administrator: None
Address: -
Telephone Number: -
Car Parking: Yes
Coach Parking: Yes
Nearest Railway Station: Wrexham
Nearest Bus Station: Wrexham
Club Shop: None
Opening Times: -
Telephone No.: -
Postal Sales: -
Nearest Police Station: Wrexham
Police Force: Wrexham Division
Police Telephone No.: (0978) 290222

DISABLED SUPPORTERS INFORMATION
Wheelchairs: Not Accommodated
Disabled Toilets: None
The Blind: No Special Facilities

ADMISSION INFO (1993/94 PRICES)
Adult Standing: Open Area - No Admission Charge
Child Standing: Open Area - No Admission Charge
Concessionary Standing: Open Area - No Charge

OTHER INFORMATION
Programme Price: 40p
Sponsors 1993/94 Season: O & J Tarpaulins,
Dymock Arms, Penley

SCHOOL   CHANGING ROOMS

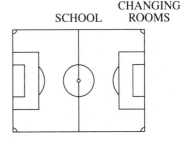

Travelling Supporters Information:
Routes: Ground is on the A539 between Wrexham & Whitchurch in the grounds of Maelor School.

PENRHYNCOCH FC

Founded: 1965	**Ground Capacity**: 1,000
Former Name(s): None	**Seating Capacity**: None
Nickname: -	**Correspondence Address**: R.J. Ellis, 4 Maes
Ground: Cae Baker, Penrhyncoch,	Laura, Aberystwyth, Dyfed SY23 2AU
Aberystwyth, Dyfed	**Contact Tel. No.**: (0970) 617171
Ground Tel. No.: (0970) 828992	**FAX Number**: None
Pitch Size: 113 × 75yds	**Colours**: Shirts - Yellow
Record Attendance: Not Known	Shorts - Blue

GENERAL INFORMATION
Supporters Club Administrator: None
Address: -
Telephone Number: -
Car Parking: At Social Club
Coach Parking: At Social Club
Nearest Railway Station: Aberystwyth
Nearest Bus Station: Aberystwyth
Club Shop: None
Opening Times: -
Telephone No.: -
Postal Sales: -
Nearest Police Station: Aberystwyth
Police Force: Dyfed/Powys
Police Telephone No.: (0970) 612791

DISABLED SUPPORTERS INFORMATION
Wheelchairs: Accommodated
Disabled Toilets: None
The Blind: No Special Facilities

ADMISSION INFO (1993/94 PRICES)
Adult Standing: £1.00
Child Standing: 50p
Concessionary Standing: 50p

OTHER INFORMATION
Programme Price: 25p
Sponsors 1993/94 Season: Jewson

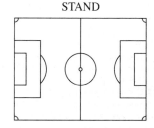

STAND

Travelling Supporters Information:
Routes: From the North: Take A487 from Machynlleth, through Talybont. Go through Bow Street, turning left at A4157, continue for 0.25 mile. Turn left at crossroads signposted Penrhyncoch and 'Welsh Plant Breeding Station'. Follow road for 1.5 miles, bearing right at village square, and you will come to Penrhyncoch FC Social Club. Cae baker is across the road. From the East: Follow A44 from Llangurig to Aberystwyth. After going through Capel Bangor, turn right onto A4159 signposted Bow Street A4159, Machynlleth (A487). After 1.75 miles turn right at crossroads, signposted Penrhyncoch and Welsh Plant Breeding Station. Then as North.

RHAYADER TOWN FC

Founded: 1879
Former Name(s): None
Nickname: 'Thin Red Line'
Ground: The Weirglodd, Rhayader, Powys
Ground Tel. No.: None
Pitch Size: 120 × 70yds
Record Attendance: 1,200
Ground Capacity: 1,500

Seating Capacity: 130
Correspondence Address: P.R. Woosnam, "Highlands", St. Harmon Road, Rhayader, Powys LD6 5PN
Contact Tel. No.: (0597) 811286
FAX Number: None
Colours: Shirts - Red & White
Shorts - Red

GENERAL INFORMATION
Supporters Club Administrator: -
Address: c/o Club Secretary
Telephone Number: -
Car Parking: At Ground
Coach Parking: At Ground
Nearest Railway Station: Llandrindod Wells
Nearest Bus Station: Llandrindod Wells
Club Shop: None
Opening Times: -
Telephone No.: -
Postal Sales: Yes
Nearest Police Station: East Street, Rhayader
Police Force: Dyfed/Powys
Police Telephone No.: (0597) 822227

DISABLED SUPPORTERS INFORMATION
Wheelchairs: Accommodated
Disabled Toilets: Yes
The Blind: No Special Facilities

ADMISSION INFO (1993/94 PRICES)
Adult Standing: £1.50
Adult Seating: £2.00
Child Standing: 60p
Child Seating: 60p
Concessionary Standing: -
Concessionary Seating: -

OTHER INFORMATION
Programme Price: 50p
Sponsors 1993/94 Season: T.L.P. Construction

'BILL THE COAL' STAND

MAIN STAND

Travelling Supporters Information:
Routes: From the North & South: Take A470 into Town Centre. Take Elan Valley route for 400 yards. Turn left into Water Lane. Ground is adjacent to Rugby Pitches at bottom of Water Lane. From the East and West: Follow A44 route into the Town Centre, then as North & South.

RHOS AELWYD FC

Founded: 1876 (1943 - As Rhos Aelwyd)
Former Name(s): Llanerchrugog Hall FC
(+ 10 other names!)
Nickname: -
Ground: Ponciau Park, Clarke Street, Ponciau, Wrexham
Ground Tel. No.: -
Pitch Size: 120 × 80yds
Record Attendance: 950 (1974)

Ground Capacity: 3,000
Seating Capacity: None
Correspondence Address: D. Parry, "Penrallt" Queen Street, Rhosllanerchrugog, Wrexham LL14 1PY
Contact Tel. No.: (0978) 845148
FAX Number: -
Colours: Shirts - Blue
　　　　　Shorts - Blue

GENERAL INFORMATION
Supporters Club Administrator: None
Address: -
Telephone Number: -
Car Parking: At Ground
Coach Parking: At Ground
Nearest Railway Station: Wrexham
Nearest Bus Station: Gardden Road, Rhos
Club Shop: None
Opening Times: -
Telephone No.: -
Postal Sales: -
Nearest Police Station: Rhosllannerchrugog
Police Force: North Wales
Police Telephone No.: (0978) 840023

DISABLED SUPPORTERS INFORMATION
Wheelchairs: Accommodated
Disabled Toilets: None
The Blind: No Special Facilities

ADMISSION INFO (1992/93 PRICES)
Adult Standing: £1.00 (by programme)
Child Standing: £1.00 (by programme)
Concessionary Standing: £1.00 (by programme)

OTHER INFORMATION
Programme Price: £1.00 (includes admission)
Sponsors 1993/94 Season: Various

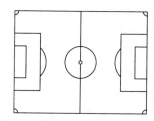

Travelling Supporters Information:
Routes: Take the A483 to Wrexham and leave at Little Chef heading for Johnstown and Ruabon. Turn right at War Memorial by New Inn and pass Fire Station. Turn right at Horse & Jockey into Chapel Street then left into Clarke Street, Ground is on left opposite the School.

RHYL FC

Founded: 1883	**Ground Capacity**: 4,000
Former Name(s): Rhyl Athletic FC	**Seating Capacity**: 200
Nickname: 'Lilywhites'	**Correspondence Address**: J. Tinston, 16 Kinnard Drive, Rhyl, Clwyd
Ground: Belle Vue, Grange Road, Rhyl, Clwyd	
Ground Tel. No.: (0745) 338237	**Contact Tel. No.**: (0745) 338305
Pitch Size: 110 × 75yds	**FAX Number**: None
Record Attendance: 10,000 vs Cardiff City 1952/53	**Colours**: Shirts - White Shorts - White

GENERAL INFORMATION
Supporters Club Administrator: None
Address: -
Telephone Number: -
Car Parking: At Ground
Coach Parking: At Ground
Nearest Railway Station: Rhyl
Nearest Bus Station: Rhyl Town Centre
Club Shop: Yes
Opening Times: Matchdays Only
Telephone No.: (0745) 338327
Postal Sales: No
Nearest Police Station: Rhyl
Police Force: North Wales
Police Telephone No.: (0745) 343898

DISABLED SUPPORTERS INFORMATION
Wheelchairs: Accommodated
Disabled Toilets: Yes
The Blind: No Special Facilities

ADMISSION INFO (1993/94 PRICES)
Adult Standing: £2.00
Adult Seating: £2.00
Child Standing: £1.00
Child Seating: £1.00
Concessionary Standing: £1.00
Concessionary Seating: £1.00

OTHER INFORMATION
Programme Price: 50p
Sponsors 1993/94 Season: -

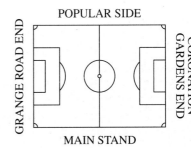

Travelling Supporters Information:
Routes: Take the A55 Expressway to the Rhyl turn-off and follow signs through Rhuddlan. Follow signs for 'Sun Centre' along Pendyffryn Road and turn left at junction. Ground is 200 yards on left.

RUTHIN TOWN FC

Founded: 1951
Former Name(s): Ruthin British Legion FC
Nickname: 'The Blues'
Ground: Memorial Playing Fields, Parc-y-Dre, Ruthin, Clwyd
Ground Tel. No.: (08242) 2766
Pitch Size: 110 × 75yds
Record Attendance: 2,000

Ground Capacity: 2,000
Seating Capacity: None
Correspondence Address: B. Lewis, 40 Maeshafod, Ruthin, Clwyd   LL15 1LS
Contact Tel. No.: (0824) 702828
FAX Number: None
Colours: Shirts - Blue & White
                 Shorts - Blue

GENERAL INFORMATION
Supporters Club Administrator: -
Address: c/o Club
Telephone Number: (0824) 702766
Car Parking: At Ground
Coach Parking: At Ground
Nearest Railway Station: Rhyl
Nearest Bus Station: Rhyl
Club Shop: None
Opening Times: -
Telephone No.: -
Postal Sales: Yes
Nearest Police Station: Ruthin (1 mile)
Police Force: North Wales
Police Telephone No.: (0824) 702041

DISABLED SUPPORTERS INFORMATION
Wheelchairs: Accommodated
Disabled Toilets: None
The Blind: No Special Facilities

ADMISSION INFO (1993/94 PRICES)
Adult Standing: £1.00
Child Standing: 50p
Concessionary Standing: 50p

OTHER INFORMATION
Programme Price: 50p
Sponsors 1993/94 Season: Snowdonia Windows, Lewis Electrics, Sam Roberts, R.W. Edwards & Sons, Donmac

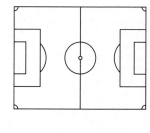

Travelling Supporters Information:
Routes: Ground is situated on Park Road (A494), Ruthin at the rear of the Fire Station.

WELSHPOOL TOWN FC

Founded: 1878	**Seating Capacity**: 120
Former Name(s): -	**Correspondence Address**: J.A. Bartley, 24
Nickname: 'Maes y Dre'	Bryn Glas, Welshpool, Powys SY21 7TL
Ground: Maesydre, Welshpool, Powys	**Contact Tel. No.**: (0938) 552131
Ground Tel. No.: None	**FAX Number**: -
Pitch Size: 108 × 72yds	**Colours**: Shirts - White
Record Attendance: Not Known	Shorts - Black
Ground Capacity: 1,500	

GENERAL INFORMATION
Supporters Club Administrator: None
Address: -
Telephone Number: -
Car Parking: At Ground
Coach Parking: At Ground
Nearest Railway Station: Welshpool (2 mins)
Nearest Bus Station: Welshpool (5 mins)
Club Shop: None
Opening Times: -
Telephone No.: -
Postal Sales: -
Nearest Police Station: Welshpool
Police Force: Dyfed/Powys
Police Telephone No.: -

DISABLED SUPPORTERS INFORMATION
Wheelchairs: Accommodated
Disabled Toilets: None
The Blind: No Special Facilities

ADMISSION INFO (1993/94 PRICES)
Adult Standing: £1.00
Adult Seating: £1.00
Child Standing: 50p
Child Seating: 50p
Concessionary Standing: 50p
Concessionary Seating: 50p

OTHER INFORMATION
Programme Price: -
Sponsors 1993/94 Season: -

STAND

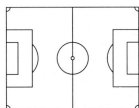

Travelling Supporters Information:
Routes: Ground is situated on the south side of Welshpool Town Centre.

WREXHAM AFC RESERVES

Founded: 1873
Former Name(s): None
Nickname: 'Robins'
Ground: Racecourse Ground, Mold Road, Wrexham, Clwyd
Ground Tel. No.: (0978) 262129
Pitch Size: 111 × 71yds
Record Attendance: 34,445 (26/1/57)

Ground Capacity: 11,500
Seating Capacity: 5,026
Correspondence Address: c/o Club
Contact Tel. No.: -
FAX Number: (0978) 357821
Colours: Shirts - Red
Shorts - White

GENERAL INFORMATION
Supporters Club Administrator: None
Address: -
Telephone Number: -
Car Parking: Town Car Parks Nearby
Coach Parking: -
Nearest Railway Station: Wrexham General (adjacent)
Nearest Bus Station: Wrexham
Club Shop: At Promotions Office
Opening Times: Matchdays Only
Telephone No.: (0978) 352536
Postal Sales: Yes
Nearest Police Station: Bodhyfryd (HQ) (1 mile)
Police Force: Wrexham Division
Police Telephone No.: (0978) 290222

DISABLED SUPPORTERS INFORMATION
Wheelchairs: Accommodated in Disabled Section
Disabled Toilets: None
The Blind: No Special Facilities

ADMISSION INFO (1993/94 PRICES)
Adult Standing: £1.00
Adult Seating: £1.50
Child Standing: £1.00
Child Seating: £1.00
Concessionary Standing: £1.00
Concessionary Seating: £1.00

OTHER INFORMATION
Programme Price: 20p
Sponsors 1993/94 Season: Wrexham Lager

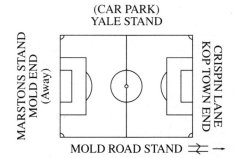

Travelling Supporters Information:
Routes: From North & West: Take A483 and Wrexham Bypass to junction with A541. Branch left and at roundabout follow Wrexham signs into Mold Road; From South & East: Take A525 or A534 into Wrexham then follow A541 signs into Mold Road.

ABERAMAN ATHLETIC FC

Founded: 1892
Former Name(s): None
Nickname: 'Aber'
Ground: Aberaman Park, Aberaman, Aberdare, Mid Glam.
Ground Tel. No.: None
Pitch Size: 115 × 75yds
Record Attendance: 10,000 (During WW2)

Ground Capacity: 2,000
Seating Capacity: None
Correspondence Address: B. Fear, 28 Mostyn Street, Abercwmboi, Aberdare, Mid Glam.
Contact Tel. No.: (0443) 472858
FAX Number: None
Colours: Shirts - Blue
Shorts - Blue

GENERAL INFORMATION
Supporters Club Administrator: None
Address: -
Telephone Number: -
Car Parking: At Ground
Coach Parking: At Ground
Nearest Railway Station: Aberdare
Nearest Bus Station: Aberdare
Club Shop: None
Opening Times: -
Telephone No.: -
Postal Sales: -
Nearest Police Station: Aberdare
Police Force: Mid Glamorgan
Police Telephone No.: -

DISABLED SUPPORTERS INFORMATION
Wheelchairs: Accommodated
Disabled Toilets: None
The Blind: No Special Facilities

ADMISSION INFO (1993/94 PRICES)
Adult Standing: £1.00 (by programme)
Child Standing: £1.00 (by programme)
Concessionary Standing: None

OTHER INFORMATION
Programme Price: £1.00 (including admission)
Sponsors 1993/94 Season: Farrells Homecare Centre

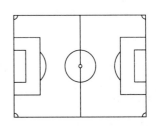

Travelling Supporters Information:
Routes: Exit M4 junction 22 and take A470 northbound. leave A470 at signs for Mountain Ash and at lights on rail bridge turn right. Proceed along this road for approximately 2 miles and grounds on right new Kwik Save Store.

ABERGAVENNY THURSDAYS FC

Founded: 1900
Former Name(s): Abergavenny Rangers FC
Nickname: 'Thursdays'
Ground: Pen Y Pound Stadium, Pen Y Pound, Abergavenny, Gwent
Ground Tel. No.: (0873) 853906
Pitch Size: 120 × 80yds
Record Attendance: 7,000
Ground Capacity: 5,000

Seating Capacity: 500
Correspondence Address: D.J. Morris, 48 Richmond Road, Abergavenny, Gwent NP7 5RE
Contact Tel. No.: (0873) 854730
FAX Number: None
Colours: Shirts - White
Shorts - White

GENERAL INFORMATION
Supporters Club Administrator: None
Address: -
Telephone Number: -
Car Parking: At Ground
Coach Parking: At Ground
Nearest Railway Station: Abergavenny
Nearest Bus Station: Abergavenny
Club Shop: None
Opening Times: -
Telephone No.: -
Postal Sales: -
Nearest Police Station: Abergavenny
Police Force: Gwent
Police Telephone No.: (0873) 852273

DISABLED SUPPORTERS INFORMATION
Wheelchairs: Accommodated
Disabled Toilets: None
The Blind: No Special Facilities

ADMISSION INFO (1993/94 PRICES)
Adult Standing: £2.00
Adult Seating: £2.00
Child Standing: £1.00
Child Seating: £1.00
Concessionary Standing: -
Concessionary Seating: -

OTHER INFORMATION
Programme Price: 50p
Sponsors 1993/94 Season: -
Social Club Phone No.: (0873) 853906

MAIN STAND

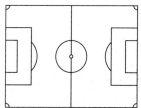

Travelling Supporters Information:
Routes: A465 follow town centre signs, one way system. Pen Y Pound is turning off ring road at Northern end of town centre. On foot from station, walk through town, turn right into Park Road, left into Pen Y Pound Road.

AMMANFORD TOWN AFC

Founded: 1991 (amalgamation of Ammanford Town FC & Ammanford Athletic FC)
Former Name(s): Betws FC
Nickname: 'The Town'
Ground: Betws Sports Club, Rice Road, Betws, Ammanford, Dyfed
Ground Tel. No.: (0269) 592407
Pitch Size: 105 × 75yds
Record Attendance: 4,000

Ground Capacity: 4,000
Seating Capacity: 450
Correspondence Address: W.J. Thomas, 142 Hendre Road, Capel Hendre, Ammanford SA18 3LE
Contact Tel. No.: (0269) 843712
FAX Number: -
Colours: Shirts - Black & White Hoops
Shorts - Black

GENERAL INFORMATION
Supporters Club Administrator: -
Address: c/o Club Secretary
Telephone Number: (0269) 843712
Car Parking: At Ground
Coach Parking: At Ground
Nearest Railway Station: Ammanford
Nearest Bus Station: Ammanford
Club Shop: None
Opening Times: -
Telephone No.: -
Postal Sales: -
Nearest Police Station: Ammanford
Police Force: Dyfed/Powys
Police Telephone No.: (0269) 592222

DISABLED SUPPORTERS INFORMATION
Wheelchairs: Accommodated
Disabled Toilets: None
The Blind: No Special Facilities

ADMISSION INFO (1993/94 PRICES)
Adult Standing: £1.30   (by programme)
Adult Seating: £1.30   (by programme)
Child Standing: £1.30   (by programme)
Child Seating: £1.30   (by programme)
Concessionary Standing: £1.00   (by programme)
Concessionary Seating: £1.00   (by programme)

OTHER INFORMATION
Programme Price: £1.30 (includes admission)
Sponsors 1993/94 Season: -

STAND

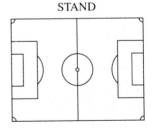

Travelling Supporters Information:
Routes: At the end of the M4 take the A483 then after about 5 miles turn right at traffic lights towards Betws. Ground is in Rice Road, Betws and is very hard to find.

BARRY TOWN AFC

Founded: 1912	**Ground Capacity**: 5,000
Former Name(s): Barri Town FC	**Seating Capacity**: 1,600
Nickname: 'The Linnetts'	**Correspondence Address**: A Whelan, 166
Ground: Jenner Park, Barry, S. Glamorgan,	Jenner Road, Barry, South Glamorgan
CF6 7BG	**Contact Tel. No.**: (0446) 737188
Ground Tel. No.: -	**FAX Number**: -
Pitch Size: 105 × 75yds	**Colours**: Shirts - Green
Record Attendance: Not Known	Shorts - Blue

GENERAL INFORMATION
Supporters Club Administrator: -
Address: -
Telephone Number: -
Car Parking: At Ground
Coach Parking: At Ground
Nearest Railway Station: Barry
Nearest Bus Station: Barry
Club Shop: Yes
Opening Times: Matchdays Only
Telephone No.: -
Postal Sales: -
Nearest Police Station: Barry
Police Force: South Glamorgan
Police Telephone No.: -

DISABLED SUPPORTERS INFORMATION
Wheelchairs: Accommodated
Disabled Toilets: None
The Blind: No Special Facilities

ADMISSION INFO (1993/94 PRICES)
Adult Standing: £1.50 (by programme)
Adult Seating: £1.50 (by programme)
Child Standing: £1.50 (by programme)
Child Seating: £1.50 (by programme)
Concessionary Standing: -
Concessionary Seating: -

OTHER INFORMATION
Programme Price: £1.50 (includes admission)
Sponsors 1993/94 Season: -

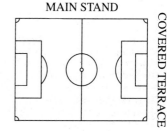

MAIN STAND

COVERED TERRACE

Travelling Supporters Information:
Routes: Exit M4 at junction 33 and follow A 4050 to Barry for Jenner Park.

BLAENRHONDDA AFC

Founded: 1934	**Ground Capacity**: 2,500
Former Name(s): None	**Seating Capacity**: None
Nickname: -	**Correspondence Address**: G. Davies, 60 Elizabeth Street, Pentre, Mid Glam.
Ground: Blaenrhondda Park, Blaenrhondda, Mid Glam.	
Ground Tel. No.: None	**Contact Tel. No.**: (0443) 433901
Pitch Size: 105 × 78yds	**FAX Number**: None
Record Attendance: 1,000	**Colours**: Shirts - Blue Shorts - Blue

GENERAL INFORMATION
Supporters Club Administrator: -
Address: c/o Club Secretary (above)
Telephone Number: (0443) 433901
Car Parking: Street Parking
Coach Parking: Bus Terminus, Blaenrhondda
Nearest Railway Station: Treherbert
Nearest Bus Station: None
Club Shop: None
Opening Times: -
Telephone No.: -
Postal Sales: -
Nearest Police Station: Ton Pentre
Police Force: South Wales
Police Telephone No.: -

DISABLED SUPPORTERS INFORMATION
Wheelchairs: Accommodated
Disabled Toilets: None
The Blind: No Special Facilities

ADMISSION INFO (1993/94 PRICES)
Adult Standing: £1.00 (by programme)
Child Standing: 50p (by programme)
Concessionary Standing: 50p (by programme)

OTHER INFORMATION
Programme Price: No Charge - part of Admission
Sponsors 1993/94 Season: W.L. Transport

```
                    TERRACE
      ┌─────────────────────────────────┐
    T │                                 │ T
    E │                                 │ E
    R │          (pitch diagram)        │ R
    R │                                 │ R
    A │                                 │ A
    C │                                 │ C
    E └─────────────────────────────────┘ E
             COVERED STAND
```

Travelling Supporters Information:
Routes: Exit M4 at junction 34 and take the A4119 past Topypandy, then take the A4061 into the Rhondda Valley. Blaenrhondda is on the left after Treherbert.

BRECON CORINTHIANS FC

Founded: 1940
Former Name(s): None
Nickname: 'Corries'
Ground: Rich Field, The Watton, Brecon, Powys
Ground Tel. No.: (0874) 624033
Pitch Size: 111 × 72yds
Record Attendance: Not Known

Ground Capacity: 6,000
Seating Capacity: 80
Correspondence Address: T. Harley, 20 Charles Street, The Watton, Brecon LD3 7HF
Contact Tel. No.: (0874) 624568
FAX Number: None
Colours: Shirts - Red
    Shorts - Red

GENERAL INFORMATION
Supporters Club Administrator: Philip Pashley
Address: 35 Coryton Close, Brecon, Powys
Telephone Number: (0874) 625543
Car Parking: Street Parking in Rich Way
Coach Parking: -
Nearest Railway Station: Merthyr Tydfil (20 miles)
Nearest Bus Station: Merthyr Tydfil (20mls)
Club Shop: None
Opening Times: -
Telephone No.: -
Postal Sales: -
Nearest Police Station: Lion Street, Brecon
Police Force: Dyfed/Powys
Police Telephone No.: (0874) 622331

DISABLED SUPPORTERS INFORMATION
Wheelchairs: Accommodated
Disabled Toilets: None (Hope to build some 1993/94)
The Blind: No Special Facilities

ADMISSION INFO (1993/94 PRICES)
Adult Standing: £1.50 (by programme)
Adult Seating: £2.50 (by programme)
Child Standing: Free
Child Seating: Free
Concessionary Standing: £1.50 (by programme)
Concessionary Seating: £1.50 (by programme)

OTHER INFORMATION
Programme Price: £1.50 (includes admission)
Sponsors 1993/94 Season: Welsh Water & Mount Pleasant Dairy

CLUBHOUSE

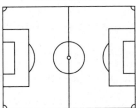

Travelling Supporters Information:
Routes: Take the main road into the Town Centre and carry on through traffic lights. After Zebra crossing turn 2nd right into Rich Way and ground is at the end of the road.

BRIDGEND TOWN FC

Founded: 1954
Former Name(s): Bridgend Vics FC
Nickname: None
Ground: Coychurch Road, Bridgend, Mid Glamorgan
Ground Tel. No.: (0656) 655097
Pitch Size: 112 × 75yds
Record Attendance: 5,000
Ground Capacity: 5,000

Seating Capacity: 200
Correspondence Address: R. Warner, 1 Heol Treharne, Coytrahen, Bridgend, Mid Glam. CF32 0DS
Contact Tel. No.: (0656) 720618
FAX Number: None
Colours: Shirts - Sky Blue
Shorts - Navy Blue

GENERAL INFORMATION
Supporters Club Administrator: K.Rowlands
Address: 23 Cowbridge Road, Bridgend
Telephone Number: (0656) 663349
Car Parking: At Ground
Coach Parking: At Ground
Nearest Railway Station: Bridgend (0.25 ml)
Nearest Bus Station: Bridgend
Club Shop: None
Opening Times: -
Telephone No.: -
Postal Sales: -
Nearest Police Station: Bridgend
Police Force: South Wales
Police Telephone No.: (0656) 655555

DISABLED SUPPORTERS INFORMATION
Wheelchairs: Accommodated
Disabled Toilets: Yes
The Blind: No Special Facilities

ADMISSION INFO (1993/94 PRICES)
Adult Standing: £1.50
Adult Seating: £1.50
Child Standing: 75p
Child Seating: 75p
Concessionary Standing: £1.00
Concessionary Seating: £1.00

OTHER INFORMATION
Programme Price: 50p
Sponsors 1993/94 Season: City Electrical Factors

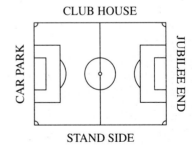

Travelling Supporters Information:
Routes: Exit M4 junction 35 and bear left at 1st roundabout. At 2nd roundabout take 3rd exit. Go under bridge, take third turning right, just before traffic lights. Ground is on the right.

CAERAU FC

Founded: 1901	**Ground Capacity**: 400
Former Name(s): Caerau Athletic FC	**Seating Capacity**: -
Nickname: -	**Correspondence Address**: David Lewis, 19A
Ground: Humphreys Terrace, Caerau, Maesteg	Hermon Road, Caerau, Nr. Bridgend CF34 0ST
Mid Glamorgan	**Contact Tel. No.**: (0656) 734388
Ground Tel. No.: (0633) 420074	**FAX Number**: -
Pitch Size: 108 × 78yds	**Colours**: Shirts - Red
Record Attendance: Cardiff City 1947	Shorts - Red

GENERAL INFORMATION
Supporters Club Administrator: None
Address: -
Telephone Number: -
Car Parking: At Ground
Coach Parking: At Ground
Nearest Railway Station: Maesteg
Nearest Bus Station: Maesteg
Club Shop: None
Opening Times: -
Telephone No.: -
Postal Sales: -
Nearest Police Station: Caerau
Police Force: South Wales
Police Telephone No.: -

DISABLED SUPPORTERS INFORMATION
Wheelchairs: Accommodated
Disabled Toilets: None
The Blind: No Special Facilities

ADMISSION INFO (1993/94 PRICES)
Adult Standing: 50p (by programme)
Child Standing: 50p (by programme)
Concessionary Standing: 50p (by programme)

OTHER INFORMATION
Programme Price: 50p (includes admission)
Sponsors 1993/94 Season: -

COVERED TERRACE

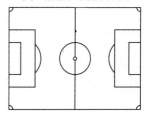

Travelling Supporters Information:
Routes: Exit M4 junction 36 and follow signs for Maesteg (A4063). Follow the road through Maesteg/ Natfyllon to Caerau. Ground is in centre of Caerau.

CAERLEON FC

Founded: 1889
Former Name(s): -
Nickname: -
Ground: Cold Bath Road, Caerleon, Gwent
Ground Tel. No.: (0633) 420074
Pitch Size: 117 × 74yds
Record Attendance: 1,000
Ground Capacity: 1,200
Seating Capacity: None

Correspondence Address: K. Alden, 2 Conifer Close, Caerleon, Gwent NP6 1RH
Contact Tel. No.: (0633) 420367
FAX Number: None
Colours: Shirts - Green
Shorts - White

GENERAL INFORMATION
Supporters Club Administrator: -
Address: -
Telephone Number: -
Car Parking: Yes
Coach Parking: Yes
Nearest Railway Station: Newport
Nearest Bus Station: Newport
Club Shop: None
Opening Times: -
Telephone No.: -
Postal Sales: -
Nearest Police Station: Caerleon
Police Force: Gwent
Police Telephone No.: -

DISABLED SUPPORTERS INFORMATION
Wheelchairs: Accommodated
Disabled Toilets: None
The Blind: No Special Facilities

ADMISSION INFO (1993/94 PRICES)
Adult Standing: £1.00
Child Standing: 50p
Concessionary Standing: 50p

OTHER INFORMATION
Programme Price: 50p
Sponsors 1993/94 Season: Various

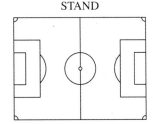

Travelling Supporters Information:
Routes: Exit M4 junction 25 and follow signs for Caerleon. In Caerleon at junction of Lodge Road turn left into Cold Bath Road for ground.

CALDICOT TOWN FC

Founded: 1953
Former Name(s): Caldicot Playing Fields FC
Nickname: 'The Town'
Ground: Jubilee Way, Caldicot, Gwent
Ground Tel. No.: (0291) 423519
Pitch Size: 110 × 75yds
Record Attendance: 600
Ground Capacity: 1,500

Seating Capacity: None
Correspondence Address: G. Lewis, "Talfan"
83 Newport Road, Caldicot, Newport NP6 4BS
Contact Tel. No.: (0291) 422035
FAX Number: None
Colours: Shirts - Yellow
Shorts - Black

GENERAL INFORMATION
Supporters Club Administrator:
Mrs P. McBride
Address: 7 Churchfield Avenue, Caldicot, Gwent
Telephone Number: (0291) 420433
Car Parking: At Ground
Coach Parking: At Ground
Nearest Railway Station: Caldicot Halt
Nearest Bus Station: Caldicot Cross
Club Shop: None
Opening Times: -
Telephone No.: -
Postal Sales: Yes
Nearest Police Station: Chepstow Road, Caldicot
Police Force: Gwent
Police Telephone No.: (0291) 430999

DISABLED SUPPORTERS INFORMATION
Wheelchairs: Accommodated
Disabled Toilets: None
The Blind: No Special Facilities

ADMISSION INFO (1993/94 PRICES)
Adult Standing: £1.50
Child Standing: 75p
Concessionary Standing: -

OTHER INFORMATION
Programme Price: 20p
Sponsors 1993/94 Season: -

JUBILEE WAY
CAR PARK

SANDY LANE
CLUBHOUSE

OPEN TERRACE

Travelling Supporters Information:
Routes: Exit M4 junction 23 Magor turn-off and follow signs for Caldicot (4-5 miles). Proceed into town centre then turn left at traffic lights and ground is 0.5 mile on left.

CARDIFF CIVIL SERVICE FC

Founded: 1963	**Ground Capacity**: 2,000
Former Name(s): St. Clair's FC	**Seating Capacity**: None
Nickname: 'Saints'	**Correspondence Address**: R.A. Fry, 30 Flax-
Ground: Sanatorium Road Playing Fields,	land Avenue, Heath, Cardiff CF4 3NT
Leckwith, Cardiff	**Contact Tel. No.**: (0222) 619192
Ground Tel. No.: (0222) 341181	**FAX Number**: None
Pitch Size: 110 × 75yds	**Colours**: Shirts - Green & White Hoops
Record Attendance: 800 v Cardiff City (1990)	Shorts - White

GENERAL INFORMATION

Supporters Club Administrator:
Tim Johnson
Address: Celtic View, Harbour Road, Barry, S. Glam.
Telephone Number: (0446) 734050
Car Parking: At Ground
Coach Parking: At Ground
Nearest Railway Station: Cardiff Central
Nearest Bus Station: Cardiff Central
Club Shop: Yes
Opening Times: Matchdays Only
Telephone No.: -
Postal Sales: via Club Secretary
Nearest Police Station: Canton (Cowbridge Road)
Police Force: South Wales
Police Telephone No.: (0222) 222111

DISABLED SUPPORTERS INFORMATION

Wheelchairs: Accommodated
Disabled Toilets: None
The Blind: No Special Facilities

ADMISSION INFO (1993/94 PRICES)

Adult Standing: £1.00
Child Standing: 50p
Concessionary Standing: 50p

OTHER INFORMATION

Programme Price: 50p
Sponsors 1993/94 Season: Bect Builders

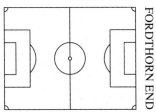

CLUBHOUSE
BECT STAND
FORDTHORN END

Travelling Supporters Information:

Routes: From North: Take A470 to junction with Cardiff by-pass then take 3rd exit at roundabout onto A48 to Port Talbot. After 2 miles take first exit at roundabout onto A4161 Cowbridge Road, turn right into Leckwith Road then right again into Broad Street. After 0.5 mile turn left before bridge for ground. From East: Exit M4 take A48 to Cardiff by-pass (then as North). From West: Take A4161 Cowbridge Road (then as North).
Bus Routes: Service Nº 2 from City Centre to Ninian Park - 0.75 mile walk from there.

FERNDALE ATHLETIC FC

Founded: 1945
Former Name(s): None
Nickname: 'Athletic'
Ground: Recreation Ground, Maerdy, Rhondda, Mid Glamorgan
Ground Tel. No.: (0443) 732607
Pitch Size: 112 × 72yds
Record Attendance: 5,600 (1957) Darran Park

Ground Capacity: 2,500
Seating Capacity: -
Correspondence Address: G.T. Lewis, Dan-Yr-Allt, Brown Street, Ferndale CF43 4SF
Contact Tel. No.: (0443) 730201
FAX Number: None
Colours: Shirts - Amber
Shorts - Black

GENERAL INFORMATION
Supporters Club Administrator: None
Address: -
Telephone Number: -
Car Parking: At Ground
Coach Parking: At Ground
Nearest Railway Station: Porth
Nearest Bus Station: Porth
Club Shop: None
Opening Times: -
Telephone No.: -
Postal Sales: -
Nearest Police Station: Ton Pentre
Police Force: South Wales
Police Telephone No.: (0443) 434222

DISABLED SUPPORTERS INFORMATION
Wheelchairs: Accommodated but no access to stand
Disabled Toilets: None
The Blind: No Special Facilities

ADMISSION INFO (1993/94 PRICES)
Adult Standing: £1.00
Child Standing: 70p
Concessionary Standing: 70p

OTHER INFORMATION
Programme Price: 25p
Sponsors 1993/94 Season: Cuddy Plant Hire

PAVILION
STAND

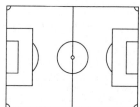

Travelling Supporters Information:
Routes: Exit M4 junction 32 and follow signs for Merthyr (A470). Carry along A470 to Porth. From Porth follow signs for Ferndale/Aberdare. Ground is situated 1.5 miles behind Ferndale on Aberdare route, turn right after British Legion, Maerdy.

LLANWERN FC

Founded: 1963
Former Name(s): Spencer Works FC
Nickname: -
Ground: B.S. Llanwern Works, Sports Ground, Tower Park, Spytty Way, Newport, Gwent
Ground Tel. No.: (0633) 273790
Pitch Size: 110 × 76yds
Record Attendance: Approx. 600 vs Newport AFC 1989

Ground Capacity: 2000
Seating Capacity: None
Correspondence Address: John Fitzgerald, 3 Lansdowne Road, Gaer, Newport, Gwent NP9 3FZ
Contact Tel. No.: (0633) 257319
FAX Number: -
Colours: Shirts - Royal Navy
Shorts - White

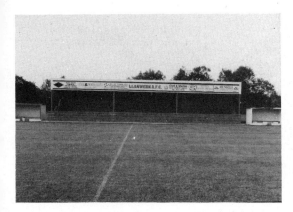

GENERAL INFORMATION
Supporters Club Administrator: None
Address: -
Telephone Number: -
Car Parking: At Ground
Coach Parking: At Ground
Nearest Railway Station: Newport
Nearest Bus Station: Newport
Club Shop: None
Opening Times: -
Telephone No.: -
Postal Sales: -
Nearest Police Station: Maindy
Police Force: Gwent
Police Telephone No.: -

DISABLED SUPPORTERS INFORMATION
Wheelchairs: Accommodated
Disabled Toilets: None
The Blind: No Special Facilities

ADMISSION INFO (1993/94 PRICES)
Adult Standing: £1.00   (by programme)
Child Standing: Free
Concessionary Standing: £1.00   (by programme)

OTHER INFORMATION
Programme Price: £1.00
Sponsors 1993/94 Season: Delta Office Supplies

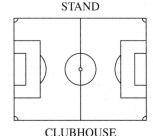

STAND

CLUBHOUSE

Travelling Supporters Information:
Routes: Exit M4 junction 24 and take A455. At 2nd roundabout exit 1st left then filter left at lights on dual carriageway and ground is straight on.

MORRISTON TOWN FC

Founded: 1926
Former Name(s): Grove Mission FC & Midland Athletic FC
Nickname: None
Ground: Dingle Road, Morriston, Swansea, West Glamorgan
Ground Tel. No.: (0792) 702033
Pitch Size: 104 × 74yds
Record Attendance: Approx 600 vs Swansea

Ground Capacity: 1,000
Seating Capacity: None
Correspondence Address: Linford Owens, 33 Heol Maes-Y-Glenen, Morriston SA6 6TU
Contact Tel. No.: (0792) 796640
FAX Number: None
Colours: Shirts - Red
Shorts - Black

GENERAL INFORMATION
Supporters Club Administrator: None
Address: -
Telephone Number: -
Car Parking: At Ground
Coach Parking: At Ground
Nearest Railway Station: Swansea
Nearest Bus Station: Swansea
Club Shop: None
Opening Times: -
Telephone No.: -
Postal Sales: -
Nearest Police Station: Morriston
Police Force: South Wales
Police Telephone No.: (0792) 771294

DISABLED SUPPORTERS INFORMATION
Wheelchairs: Accommodated
Disabled Toilets: None
The Blind: No Special Facilities

ADMISSION INFO (1993/94 PRICES)
Adult Standing: £1.00 (by programme)
Child Standing: £1.00 (by programme)
Concessionary Standing: £1.00 (by programme)

OTHER INFORMATION
Programme Price: £1.00 (includes admission)
Sponsors 1993/94 Season: Various

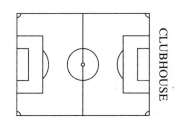

Travelling Supporters Information:
Routes: Exit M4 at junction 45 for Swansea and take 2nd exit at roundabout bearing left. Ground is 0.5 mile along this road on the right behind houses.

PEMBROKE BOROUGH FC

Founded: 1906
Former Name(s): Dock Stars FC
Nickname: 'Magpies'
Ground: London Road, Pembroke Dock, Dyfed
Ground Tel. No.: (0646) 682239
Pitch Size: 110 × 72yds
Record Attendance: 2,000
Ground Capacity: 2,000

Seating Capacity: 180
Correspondence Address: P. Tallet, 6 Shropshire Road, Llanion Park, Pembroke Dock, Dyfed
Contact Tel. No.: (0646) 682234
FAX Number: None
Colours: Shirts - Black, White & Blue
Shorts - Black

GENERAL INFORMATION
Supporters Club Administrator: P. Tallet
Address: As Above
Telephone Number: (0646) 682234
Car Parking: At Ground
Coach Parking: At Ground
Nearest Railway Station: Pembroke Docks (200 yards)
Nearest Bus Station: Western Way
Club Shop: None
Opening Times: -
Telephone No.: -
Postal Sales: -
Nearest Police Station: Pembroke Dock
Police Force: Dyfed/Powys
Police Telephone No.: (0646) 681212

DISABLED SUPPORTERS INFORMATION
Wheelchairs: Accommodated
Disabled Toilets: None
The Blind: No Special Facilities

ADMISSION INFO (1993/94 PRICES)
Adult Standing: £1.00
Adult Seating: £1.00
Child Standing: 50p
Child Seating: 50p
Concessionary Standing: -
Concessionary Seating: -

OTHER INFORMATION
Programme Price: 30p
Sponsors 1993/94 Season: Nat Power

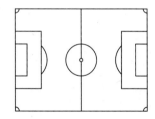

Travelling Supporters Information:
Routes: Take A477 and follow signs for Pembroke Dock. Ground is opposite Esso garage on right-hand side of road.

PONTYPRIDD TOWN AFC

Founded: 1895	**Ground Capacity**: 2,000
Former Name(s): Ynysybwl FC	**Seating Capacity**: None
Nickname: None	**Correspondence Address**: Peter Chalmers, 9
Ground: Ynysangharad Parc, Pontypridd, Mid	Silverhill Close, Cilfynydd, Pontypridd
Glamorgan	**Contact Tel. No.**: (0443) 492354
Ground Tel. No.: None	**FAX Number**: None
Pitch Size: 110 × 70yds	**Colours**: Shirts - White
Record Attendance: 200	Shorts - Blue

GENERAL INFORMATION
Supporters Club Administrator: None
Address: -
Telephone Number: -
Car Parking: Street Parking
Coach Parking: B & Q Car Park
Nearest Railway Station: Pontypridd (0.5ml)
Nearest Bus Station: Pontypridd (0.25 mile)
Club Shop: None
Opening Times: -
Telephone No.: -
Postal Sales: Yes
Nearest Police Station: Pontypridd
Police Force: South Wales
Police Telephone No.: (0443) 485356

DISABLED SUPPORTERS INFORMATION
Wheelchairs: Accommodated
Disabled Toilets: None
The Blind: No Special Facilities

ADMISSION INFO (1993/94 PRICES)
Adult Standing: £1.00   (by programme)
Child Standing: £1.00   (by programme)
Concessionary Standing: £1.00 (by programme)

OTHER INFORMATION
Programme Price: £1.00 (includes admission)
Sponsors 1993/94 Season: 4 Seasons Travel

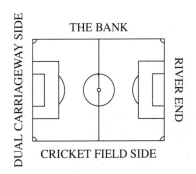

Travelling Supporters Information:
Routes: Take the A470 to Pontypridd and leave it at the Ynysybwl turn off. The ground is in a park adjacent to the A470 northbound and no cars are allowed in the park. Street parking can be found behind the Llenover Public House opposite the park.

PORT TALBOT ATHLETIC FC

Founded: 1901	**Seating Capacity**: None
Former Name(s): None	**Correspondence Address**: A. Germain, 1
Nickname: 'The Blues'	Birdsfield Cottage, Graig, Pontypridd, Mid
Ground: Victoria Road Ground, Victoria Road	Glamorgan CF37 1LE
Port Talbot SA12 6AD	**Contact Tel. No.**: (0443) 407868
Ground Tel. No.: (0639) 882465	**FAX Number**: None
Pitch Size: 118 × 70yds	**Colours**: Shirts - Blue
Record Attendance: Over 2,000	Shorts - Blue
Ground Capacity: 5,000	

GENERAL INFORMATION
Supporters Club Administrator: Pat Pearce
Address: c/o Club
Telephone Number: (0639) 882465
Car Parking: Street Parking
Coach Parking: At Ground
Nearest Railway Station: Port Talbot Parkway
Nearest Bus Station: Port Talbot Centre
Club Shop: Yes
Opening Times: Matchdays Only
Telephone No.: (0639) 882465
Postal Sales: Yes
Nearest Police Station: Station Road, Port Talbot
Police Force: South Wales
Police Telephone No.: (0639) 883101

DISABLED SUPPORTERS INFORMATION
Wheelchairs: Accommodated
Disabled Toilets: None
The Blind: No Special Facilities

ADMISSION INFO (1993/94 PRICES)
Adult Standing: £1.00
Child Standing: £1.00
Concessionary Standing: £1.00

OTHER INFORMATION
Programme Price: £1.00
Sponsors 1993/94 Season: Hawkins Securities and Selwyn Jenkins Sports

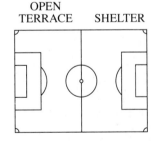

OPEN
TERRACE   SHELTER

Travelling Supporters Information:
Routes: Exit M4 junction 40 and head for town centre. Bear left at first roundabout for Aberavon beach and turn right after traffic lights at health centre into Victoria Road. Turn 2nd left after traffic lights for ground.

AFC PORTH

Founded: 1950
Former Name(s): Beatos United FC
Nickname: 'Black Dragons'
Ground: Dinas Park, Dinas, Porth, Rhondda, Mid Glamorgan
Ground Tel. No.: -
Pitch Size: 110 × 83yds
Record Attendance: Not Known
Ground Capacity: 2,000

Seating Capacity: 200
Correspondence Address: AFC Porth Social Club, 66 Hannah Street, Porth Rhondda, Mid Glamorgan   CF39 9PY
Contact Tel. No.: (0443) 688073
FAX Number: None
Colours: Shirts - Blue & Red
           Shorts - Blue

GENERAL INFORMATION
Supporters Club Administrator: None
Address: -
Telephone Number: -
Car Parking: At Ground
Coach Parking: At Ground
Nearest Railway Station: Dinas
Nearest Bus Station: Dinas
Club Shop: None
Opening Times: -
Telephone No.: -
Postal Sales: -
Nearest Police Station: Porth
Police Force: South Wales
Police Telephone No.: -

DISABLED SUPPORTERS INFORMATION
Wheelchairs: Accommodated
Disabled Toilets: None
The Blind: No Special Facilities

ADMISSION INFO (1993/94 PRICES)
Adult Standing: £1.50
Adult Seating: £1.50
Child Standing: 75p
Child Seating: 75p
Concessionary Standing: 75p
Concessionary Seating: 75p

OTHER INFORMATION
Programme Price: 50p
Sponsors 1993/94 Season: Welsh Windows, Bousfield Inks & Graphics, P. Wasley Fabrications

STAND

CHANGING ROOMS

Travelling Supporters Information:
Routes: Exit M4 junction 32 and take the A470 towards Merthyr Tydfil. Leave A470 at signs for Pontypridd (Rhondda Valley). On reaching Porth follow signs for Dinas/Tonypandy and after 3 miles ground is on right.

Konica League Season 1992/93

	ABERGAVENNY	ABERYSTWYTH	AFAN LIDO	BANGOR CITY	BRITON FERRY	CAERSWS	CONNAH'S QUAY	CONWY UNITED	CWMBRAN T.	EBBW VALE	FLINT TOWN	HAVERFORDWEST	HOLYWELL T.	INTER CARDIFF	LLANELLI	LLANIDLOES T.	MAESTEG PARK	MOLD ALEXAND.	NEWTOWN	PORTHMADOG
Abergavenny		0-1	0-6	0-1	3-4	1-2	0-2	2-1	2-2	2-2	2-2	3-1	1-3	3-2	0-0	0-2	0-0	0-2	3-1	1-1
Aberystwyth	2-0		1-0	0-2	6-0	3-2	3-1	0-2	0-2	4-1	2-0	0-2	3-1	1-3	2-2	5-1	3-1	1-1	6-1	2-2
Afan Lido	2-1	0-1		1-0	3-2	2-2	2-1	2-3	0-0	1-3	1-0	0-3	2-1	0-0	1-2	3-1	3-3	4-2	2-1	0-1
Bangor City	3-1	1-0	3-2		2-4	4-1	1-2	4-1	2-3	1-0	4-0	3-0	0-6	0-1	4-3	6-1	1-1	7-1	3-1	1-1
Briton Ferry	1-3	1-2	1-1	2-5		1-1	0-3	1-3	0-4	1-1	3-1	1-1	2-0	2-3	1-1	7-1	2-2	0-4	6-1	4-0
Caersws	1-3	5-0	2-0	2-1	0-0		0-0	2-0	1-2	0-0	3-0	1-3	0-1	1-2	2-2	0-0	3-1	5-2	1-1	0-3
Connah's Quay	2-1	1-3	5-2	0-0	1-3	2-1		1-0	0-1	5-0	4-1	2-0	4-2	1-2	0-3	1-1	3-1	1-3	4-1	0-1
Conwy United	1-0	3-1	2-2	0-2	4-2	0-0	4-3		0-1	2-0	2-1	2-1	0-0	0-1	1-0	5-2	1-0	0-4	1-1	0-0
Cwmbran Town	1-0	2-0	3-0	2-2	1-0	1-1	6-1	2-2		0-1	2-0	1-0	1-1	3-0	2-1	2-1	3-1	2-0	1-1	2-1
Ebbw Vale	3-0	3-2	5-4	1-1	10-0	5-3	3-2	1-0	0-1		1-3	2-2	0-0	2-5	1-0	3-1	2-0	1-1	5-2	1-1
Flint Town	2-0	0-2	2-0	0-3	3-1	1-2	1-3	1-1	0-0	0-2		0-1	0-2	0-2	1-1	4-1	1-2	1-1	0-3	3-1
Haverfordwest	1-2	1-3	2-3	2-2	3-1	1-3	4-0	1-3	0-5	3-0	4-3		2-0	0-1	2-1	1-1	5-2	5-3	1-2	1-2
Holywell Town	3-0	1-3	1-1	2-0	2-0	5-0	0-0	2-2	1-3	1-4	3-1	0-1		2-0	3-1	1-3	1-1	4-2	1-1	0-1
Inter Cardiff	1-0	1-2	5-2	4-0	5-1	4-1	4-0	1-0	0-0	1-2	1-1	2-3	2-0		4-1	2-1	0-0	1-0	5-1	2-1
Llanelli	1-0	1-3	0-2	1-3	1-0	0-2	1-3	1-2	0-1	4-2	1-3	1-1	0-2	1-4		4-2	3-2	2-0	3-0	0-3
Llanidloes	1-1	0-6	2-2	1-3	2-1	0-2	3-2	3-0	1-0	3-4	2-4	1-2	1-5	1-1	0-1		0-1	2-1	0-3	1-1
Maesteg Park	3-0	0-2	2-2	5-0	1-1	3-2	4-0	1-1	0-2	0-1	2-0	3-0	0-2	1-1	1-1			1-2	1-0	1-1
Mold Alexandra	3-1	1-3	1-2	3-1	1-2	2-3	2-1	2-1	1-0	0-1	1-3	3-0	1-4	0-1	1-0	4-2	1-0		4-0	0-3
Newtown	1-0	1-3	1-1	3-1	2-3	1-5	1-2	3-0	1-2	2-2	1-2	4-3	0-1	1-4	2-2	2-0	4-4	1-3		1-0
Porthmadog	9-0	3-4	0-3	0-0	0-0	3-2	2-3	0-1	0-2	3-0	2-1	1-3	2-3	2-0	1-2	2-2	2-1	3-0	2-2	

KONICA LEAGUE OF WALES 1992/93

LEAGUE TABLE FINAL

Cwmbran	38	26	9	3	69	22	87
Inter Cardiff	38	26	5	7	79	36	83
Aberystwyth Town	38	25	3	10	85	49	78
Ebbw Vale	38	19	9	10	76	61	66
Bangor City	38	19	7	12	77	58	64
Holywell Town	38	17	8	13	65	48	59
Conwy United	38	16	9	13	51	51	57
Connah's Quay Nom.	38	17	4	17	66	67	55
Porthmadog	38	14	11	13	61	49	53
Haverfordwest Cnty.	38	16	5	17	66	66	53
Caersws	38	14	10	14	64	60	52
Afan Lido	38	14	10	14	64	65	52
Mold Alexandra	38	16	4	18	63	69	*48
Llanelli	38	11	8	19	49	64	41
Maesteg Park Athletic	38	9	13	16	52	59	40
Flint Town United	38	11	6	21	47	67	39
Briton Ferry Athletic	38	10	9	19	61	87	39
Newtown	38	9	9	20	55	87	36
Llanidloes Town	38	7	9	22	48	93	30
Abergavenny Thurs.	38	7	7	24	36	76	28

* Mold Alexandra had 3 points deducted

Champions : - Cwmbran

	BRYMBO	CARNO	CEFN DRUIDS	GRESFORD ATH.	KNIGHTON T	LEX XI	LLANS'TFFRAID	MOSTYN	PENRHYNCOCH	RHAYADER T	RHOS AELWYD	RHYL	RUTHIN TOWN	WELSHPOOL T	WREXHAM RES
Brymbo		1-2	2-2	2-0	1-2	1-1	1-4	2-3	1-1	5-0	2-3	0-2	1-1	2-3	1-3
Carno	0-0		1-1	3-2	1-1	1-2	1-4	3-2	1-1	2-0	5-2	0-3	2-2	2-1	1-1
Cefn Druids	3-0	2-1		1-1	4-1	1-3	0-2	6-0	2-3	0-1	3-0	0-3	1-1	2-1	1-2
Gresford Athletic	1-3	2-4	0-1		2-1	2-3	1-2	1-0	4-1	2-1	1-2	3-2	0-2	0-3	1-2
Knighton Town	3-3	3-3	2-1	0-1		2-2	1-2	1-1	0-4	2-0	4-2	2-5	4-3	1-6	2-7
Lex XI	2-1	2-2	2-1	4-1	4-1		2-2	5-1	1-0	1-1	3-1	0-2	2-3	0-3	0-0
Llansantffraid	1-0	7-2	4-0	5-2	9-4	0-1		4-2	8-1	4-0	5-1	1-1	3-1	2-0	2-0
Mostyn	3-1	0-2	0-2	2-0	1-4	1-2	0-2		2-3	0-0	3-1	2-1	0-1	1-4	1-7
Penrhyncoch	5-1	1-2	2-1	8-2	2-3	2-2	3-5	1-0		3-1	4-4	0-2	1-2	1-5	2-0
Rhayader Town	3-2	0-0	2-4	8-2	3-2	1-5	1-2	1-2	2-2		1-2	0-5	3-2	0-2	1-0
Rhos Aelwyd	2-2	0-0	0-2	4-2	2-2	2-1	0-1	1-2	3-2	0-0		0-2	2-1	0-5	0-1
Rhyl	6-0	4-0	2-2	3-0	0-0	3-1	5-0	1-0	4-0	4-0	1-0		3-0	3-0	1-1
Ruthin Town	2-1	1-0	1-0	1-0	3-0	3-3	0-3	3-3	1-3	3-0	1-1	3-4		0-1	1-4
Welshpool Town	4-0	4-1	2-1	7-4	5-0	2-2	4-4	3-2	6-0	3-2	5-0	3-1	7-0		0-2
Wrexham Res.	4-4	7-1	4-2	1-0	3-0	3-2	0-2	2-1	6-0	5-0	6-2	4-2	5-1	1-3	

MANWEB CYMRU ALLIANCE 1992/93

LEAGUE TABLE FINAL

Llansantffraid	28	23	3	2	89	34	72
Welshpool	28	21	2	5	92	34	65
Rhyl	28	20	4	4	74	22	64
Wrexham Reserves	28	19	4	5	81	34	61
Lex XI	28	14	8	6	60	42	50
Carno	28	9	11	8	44	56	38
Cefn Druids	28	10	5	13	46	41	35
Penrhyncoch	28	10	5	13	56	71	35
Ruthin Town	28	9	7	12	43	58	34
Rhos Aelwyd	28	7	6	15	37	67	27
Knighton Town	28	7	6	15	48	82	27
Mostyn	28	7	3	18	35	64	24
Rhayader Town	28	6	5	17	32	66	23
Gresford Athletic	28	6	1	21	36	76	19
Brymbo	28	3	8	17	40	66	17

Champions : - Llansantffraid

Abacus League Division One Season 1992/93	ABERAMAN	AMMANFORD	BLAENRHONDDA	BRECON	BRIDGEND	CAERLEON	CALDICOT	CIVIL SERVICE	FERNDALE	MORRISTON	PEMBROKE	PONTYPRIDD	PORT TALBOT	TON PENTRE
Aberaman		2-2	4-0	5-1	0-4	1-3	0-0	3-1	2-4	1-4	3-0	2-1	1-2	3-2
Ammanford	1-1		2-1	3-1	1-2	3-3	1-3	0-1	1-2	1-2	4-0	1-1	2-1	4-0
Blaenrhondda	3-1	1-2		2-2	0-2	2-1	4-0	2-0	0-2	2-0	2-1	1-0	2-2	5-1
Brecon	1-0	1-1	1-3		1-3	2-3	1-3	2-2	0-3	3-3	1-6	5-1	5-6	2-1
Bridgend	0-6	2-1	3-3	7-0		4-1	1-2	3-0	0-1	2-5	1-1	1-1	2-2	5-3
Caerleon	6-0	2-0	1-0	5-1	1-3		5-3	0-1	1-2	1-0	2-0	5-2	2-0	1-2
Caldicot	1-4	2-1	0-1	0-1	1-4	1-1		0-2	3-2	1-0	2-3	1-0	0-0	3-1
Civil Service	2-3	2-1	0-3	1-0	0-2	3-1	2-0		2-4	3-1	0-3	3-0	2-1	1-0
Ferndale	3-1	3-0	2-3	1-0	4-0	5-0	1-0	0-0		5-1	5-2	4-0	5-0	5-1
Morriston	3-1	1-1	0-0	5-3	2-4	1-2	2-0	5-2	0-2		3-1	7-2	1-1	5-1
Pembroke	6-0	3-1	1-3	3-1	0-1	1-2	7-1	3-1	0-3	2-2		2-0	2-1	2-0
Pontypridd	1-0	0-0	3-3	4-1	1-1	0-1	2-2	0-2	0-0	1-6	0-0		0-1	4-0
Port Talbot	3-1	1-5	1-3	2-1	1-0	0-1	2-1	2-1	2-4	2-6	6-0	4-0		2-1
Ton Pentre	0-2	0-5	0-1	1-3	0-1	0-3	2-1	1-2	0-4	2-1	1-2	0-0	0-4	

ABACUS LEAGUE DIVISION ONE

1992/93 SEASON

Ton Pentre	26	22	1	3	71	20	67
Brecon	26	17	4	5	74	40	55
Pontypridd	26	14	9	3	53	23	51
Caldicot	26	14	4	8	50	31	46
Aberaman	26	13	3	10	54	47	42
Ammanford	26	11	7	8	38	44	40
Pembroke Borough	26	11	3	12	46	51	36
Cardiff Civil Service	26	11	2	13	40	36	35
Port Talbot	26	10	4	12	48	49	34
Morriston	26	9	5	12	46	66	32
Caerleon	26	8	2	16	36	54	26
Blaenrhondda	26	6	5	15	32	50	23
Bridgend	26	6	5	15	38	58	23
Ferndale	26	2	2	22	19	76	8

Champions : - Ton Pentre

ABACUS LEAGUE DIVISION TWO

1992/93 SEASON

AFC Porth	26	20	4	2	81	25	64
Caerau	26	16	5	5	61	30	53
Llanwern	26	15	6	5	43	22	51
Risca	26	15	4	7	44	29	49
Carmarthen	26	10	8	8	51	43	38
Taffs Well	26	11	5	10	48	42	38
Skewen	26	11	2	13	46	48	35
BP	26	9	8	9	35	41	35
Tonyrefail	26	7	9	10	38	42	30
Garw	26	6	8	12	40	55	26
Fields Park	26	7	4	15	33	43	25
Cardiff Cornes	26	7	7	12	33	69	25
Newport YMCA	26	6	3	17	37	64	21
Seven Sisters	26	4	3	19	24	61	15

Promoted : - AFC Porth, Caerau, Llanwern

ABACUS LEAGUE DIVISION THREE

1992/93 SEASON

Treowen	26	21	4	1	61	14	67
Pontyclun	26	16	5	5	58	32	53
Milford	26	15	2	9	74	36	47
Penrhiwceiber	26	13	8	5	57	44	47
Cardiff Institute HE	26	11	6	9	63	49	39
Panteg	26	10	8	8	44	39	38
Pontardawe	26	9	9	8	46	44	36
Goytre	26	11	3	12	48	49	36
Pontlottyn	26	7	9	10	35	44	30
Abercynon	26	7	8	11	35	47	29
AFC Tondu	26	6	8	12	43	60	26
Treharris	26	6	5	15	40	51	23
SW Constabulary	26	4	3	14	34	63	20
Trelewis	26	3	3	20	27	93	12

Promoted : - Treowen, Pontyclun, Milford

SEALINK STENA WELSH ALLIANCE LEAGUE

LEAGUE TABLE FINAL

Cemaes Bay	32	23	6	3	113	30	75
Llanfairpwll	32	22	4	6	73	42	70
Llangefni Town	32	21	6	5	97	45	69
Llandudno	32	21	4	7	86	41	67
Pilkingtons	32	18	6	8	78	57	60
Rhydymwyn	32	16	4	12	58	46	52
Nefyn United	32	13	8	11	61	64	47
Loco Llanberis	32	11	12	9	71	68	45
Bangor City	32	13	6	13	61	57	45
Nantlle Vale	32	12	6	14	74	79	42
Llanrwst United	32	11	5	16	58	82	38
Llandyrnog United	32	9	7	16	50	71	34
Connah's Quay Res.	32	9	6	17	47	84	33
Y Felinheli	32	7	10	15	52	64	31
Conwy United	32	6	5	21	49	78	23
Rhyl United	32	5	4	23	48	103	19
Penmaenmawr Ph.	32	3	5	24	33	104	14

Promoted : - Cemaes Bay & Llandudno

RICHARDS THE BUILDERS MID WALES LEAGUE

LEAGUE TABLE FINAL

Machynlleth	36	28	2	6	116	51	86
Morda United	36	26	4	6	85	36	82
Llandrindod Wells	36	22	4	10	108	57	70
Talgarth	36	19	10	7	80	30	67
Waterloo Rovers	36	21	4	11	80	63	67
Caersws Reserves	36	21	2	13	82	57	65
Abersytwyth T. Res.	36	19	8	9	70	59	65
Vale of Arrow	36	18	10	8	77	49	64
Berriew	36	19	5	12	68	44	62
Newtown Reserves	36	14	7	15	71	57	49
Penparcau	36	14	6	16	86	75	48
Kington Town	36	13	7	16	77	84	46
Clun Valley	36	8	11	17	31	58	35
Builth Wells	36	8	9	19	48	79	33
Presteigne St. And.	36	7	10	19	53	93	31
Knighton Town Res.	36	8	7	21	50	99	31
Penrhyncoch Res.	36	5	8	23	38	107	23
U.C.W. Aberystwyth	36	5	7	24	47	96	22
Llanidloes Town Res.	36	3	7	26	44	97	16

Relegated : - U.C.W. Aberystwyth & Llanidloes Town Reserves

REED CONSTUCTION WREXHAM AREA LEAGUE PREMIER DIVISION 1992/93

LEAGUE TABLE FINAL

Penley	26	15	7	4	63	36	52
Buckley	26	16	3	7	59	37	51
New Broughton	26	13	9	4	56	29	48
Llay Welfare	26	14	6	6	60	39	48
Marchwiel Villa	26	14	5	7	61	43	47
Lex XI Reserves	26	12	5	9	46	40	41
Chirk A.A.A.	26	11	6	9	51	41	39
Penycae	26	10	7	9	60	54	37
Llay Royal Brit. Leg.	26	8	6	12	49	46	30
Ruthin Town Res.	26	7	8	11	37	45	29
Overton Athletic	26	8	1	17	36	60	25
Corwen Amateurs	26	6	6	14	41	66	24
Treuddyn Villa	26	6	2	18	49	90	20
Castell Alun Colts	26	3	7	16	30	69	16

Promoted : - Penley

DIVISION TWO SEASON 1992/93

LEAGUE TABLE FINAL

Rhost. & Bersh. RBL	30	23	2	5	113	48	71
Ruthin Town Colts	30	18	9	3	86	34	63
Cefn Druids Colts	30	17	7	6	89	55	58
Llangollen Town	30	18	4	8	78	50	58
Chirk A.A.A. Res.	30	15	5	10	79	65	50
British Aerosp. Res.	30	14	7	9	107	82	49
Bala Town	30	11	11	8	64	55	44
O.C. Fibreglass	30	13	5	12	63	65	44
Llay Welfare Res.	30	11	7	12	57	49	40
Glynceiriog	30	11	6	13	65	73	39
Corwen Amats. Res.	30	11	5	14	60	79	38
Overton Athletic Res.	30	10	3	17	59	91	30
Llanuwchllyn	30	8	3	19	65	100	27
Penycae Reserves	30	6	4	20	58	98	22
Llay R.B.L. Reserves	30	4	5	21	47	100	17
Cast. Alun Colts Res.	30	7	3	20	45	95	15

Overton Athletic Reserves - 3 points deducted
Castell Alun Colts Reserves - 9 points deducted

DIVISION ONE SEASON 1992/93

LEAGUE TABLE FINAL

Cefn Druids Res.	30	23	4	3	107	41	73
New Brighton Villa	30	20	6	4	84	28	66
Rockwell	30	19	5	6	87	60	62
Bradley Park Rangers	30	17	4	9	79	58	55
Kelloggs	30	15	4	11	84	61	49
British Aerospace	30	15	2	13	93	57	47
Johnstown Athletic	30	16	4	10	68	66	47
New Broughton Res.	30	13	4	13	65	57	43
Kinnerton	30	11	7	12	59	64	40
Penley Reserves	30	10	7	13	65	75	37
Brymbo Reserves	30	13	3	14	64	84	36
Rhos Aelwyd Res.	30	9	6	15	56	71	33
Gresford Ath. Res.	30	9	5	16	62	80	32
J.C.B. Transmissions	30	8	6	16	65	90	30
Marchwiel Villa Res.	30	4	2	24	52	117	14
Mynydd Isa	30	2	5	23	47	128	11

Johnstown Athletic - 3 points deducted
Brymbo Reserves - 6 points deducted

UNIVERSAL CONTRACTORS SENIOR LEAGUE 1992/93

LEAGUE TABLE FINAL

Grange Quins	32	29	1	2	127	31	88
L. C. Caerau Ely	32	27	2	3	115	38	83
Trelai Y.C.	32	19	4	9	92	54	64
Lisvane Heath Horn.	32	16	6	10	71	57	56
Grange Albion	32	16	5	11	69	64	56
Maesteg Park	32	14	8	10	60	59	50
A.F.C. Llwydcoed	32	14	3	15	72	63	48
Stanleytown	32	13	4	15	68	78	43
B.P. Barry	32	12	4	16	61	71	40
Tredomen	32	11	7	14	86	103	40
Tongwynlais	32	10	6	16	58	64	39
Wenvoe Park	32	11	7	14	60	78	37
Afan Lido	32	12	6	14	43	67	34
Cogan Coronation	32	7	11	14	41	65	34
A.F.C. Porth	32	6	8	18	65	93	26
Cefn Cribwr B.C.	32	6	6	20	50	100	24
Bettws Athletic	32	5	0	27	43	116	12

Trelai Y.C. 3 points added
Lisvane Heath Hornets 2 points added
Grange Albion 3 points added
A.F.C. Llwydcoed 3 points added
Tongwynlais 3 points added
Wenvoe Park 3 points deducted
Afan Lido 8 points deducted
Cogan Coronation 2 points added
Bettws Athletic 3 points deducted

Promoted : - Grange Harlequins

B.P. LLANDARCY FC
Abacus Division Two

Year Founded: 1922
Nickname: 'The Oilers'
Former Names: None
Club Colours: Shirts - Amber
Shorts - Green
Ground Address: B.P. Sports Ground, Llandarcy, Neath
Telephone Nº: (0792) 812036
Ground Capacity: 1,000
Seating Capacity: None
Contact Address: Secretary - D. Maddock, 20 Brookfield Neath Abbey, Neath   SA10 7EG
Contact Phone Nº: (0639) 636327

CARDIFF CORINTHIANS FC
Abacus Division Two

Year Founded: 1897
Nickname: 'Corries'
Former Names: None
Club Colours: Shirts - Cardinal and Gold Quarters
Shorts - Cardinal
Ground Address: Riverside Ground, Thro' Station Road, Radyr, Nr. Cardiff
Telephone Nº: Radyr 843407
Ground Capacity: Not Known
Seating Capacity: None
Contact Address: G. Thomas, 9 Palace Road, Llandaff, Cardiff   CF5 2AF
Contact Phone Nº: (0222) 562624

CARMARTHEN TOWN FC
Abacus Division Two

Year Founded: -
Nickname: -
Former Names: -
Club Colours: Shirts - Old Gold
Shorts - Black
Ground Address: Richmond Park, Priory Street, Carmarthen, Dyfed
Telephone Nº: (0267) 232101
Ground Capacity: -
Seating Capacity: -
Contact Address: Mr. A.H. Latham, 3 Maes Dolau, Idole, Carmarthen, Dyfed   SA32 8DQ
Contact Phone Nº: (0267) 232432

FIELDS PARK PONTLLANFRAITH AFC
Abacus Division Two

Year Founded: Reformed 1964, Renamed 1992
Nickname: None
Former Names: Fields Park AFC, Pontllanfraith AFC
Club Colours: Shirts - Royal Blue
Shorts - Royal Blue
Ground Address: Islwyn Park, Pontllanfraith, Blackwood, Gwent
Telephone Nº: (0495) 224512
Ground Capacity: 2,000
Seating Capacity: 450
Contact Address: 1 William Street, Cwmfelinfach, Ymysddu, Newport, Gwent   NP1 7GY
Contact Phone Nº: (0495) 200349

GARW AFC

Year Founded: 1945
Nickname: 'Athletic'
Former Names: Garw Athletic AFC
Club Colours: Shirts - Red
             Shorts - Black
Ground Address: Blandy Park, Pontycymer, Nr. Bridgend, Mid Glam.
Telephone Nº: None
Ground Capacity: -
Seating Capacity: None
Contact Address: T.Thomas, Drosglo, 5 Victoria St., Pontycymer, Nr. Bridgend, Mid Glam CF32 8NW
Contact Phone Nº: (0656) 870411

MILFORD UNITED FC

Year Founded: 1885
Nickname: 'The Robins'
Former Names: None
Club Colours: Shirts - Red
             Shorts - White (Red & White Stockings)
Ground Address: Marble Hall Road, Milford Haven, Pembrokeshire, Dyfed
Telephone Nº: (0646) 693691
Ground Capacity: 4,000
Seating Capacity: Between 350 & 400
Contact Address: K. Lowe, 17 Milton Crescent, Pill, Milford Haven, Pembrokeshire, Dyfed SA73 2QS
Contact Phone Nº: (0646) 692194

NEWPORT Y.M.C.A. FC

Year Founded: 1971
Nickname: -
Former Names: Formed by amalgamation of Pill YMCA FC and Central YMCA FC
Club Colours: Shirts - Red
             Shorts - Black
Ground Address: Mendalgief Road, Newport, Gwent
Telephone Nº: (0633) 263387
Ground Capacity: -
Seating Capacity: -
Contact Address: Mr. R. Leonard, 14 St. David's Crescent, Park Avenue, Newport, Gwent
Contact Phone Nº: (0633) 810763

PONTYCLUN FC

Year Founded: 1896
Nickname: 'The Clun'
Former Names: None
Club Colours: Shirts - Yellow
             Shorts - Blue
Ground Address: Ivor Park, Cowbridge Road, Pontyclun, Mid Glamorgan
Telephone Nº: None
Ground Capacity: -
Seating Capacity: None
Contact Address: c/o 3 Lilac Drive, Chandlers Reach, Llantwit Farore, Mid Glamorgan CF38 2PH
Contact Phone Nº: (0443) 217305

RISCA UNITED FC
Abacus Division Two

Year Founded: 1946
Nickname: 'The Cuckoos'
Former Names: None
Club Colours: Shirts - Black & White Stripes
Shorts -Black
Ground Address: Ty-Isaf Park, Risca, Gwent
Telephone Nº: (0633) 65081?
Ground Capacity: -
Seating Capacity: None
Contact Address: Mrs Ann Luckwell (Secretary), 137 Ty-Isaf Park Avenue, Risca, Gwent NP1 6NL
Contact Phone Nº: (0633) 613434

SEVEN SISTERS FC
Abacus Division Two

Year Founded: 1946
Nickname: None
Former Names: None
Club Colours: Shirts - Yellow
Shorts - Blue
Ground Address: Welfare Ground, Church Road, Seven Sisters, Neath, West Glamorgan
Telephone Nº: None
Ground Capacity: -
Seating Capacity: None
Contact Address: c/o 1 Mary Street, Seven Sisters, Neath, West Glamorgan
Contact Phone Nº: (0639) 700121

SKEWEN ATHLETIC AFC
Abacus Division Two

Year Founded: 1932
Nickname: None
Former Names: Garthmoor FC (from 1932), Neath Athletic FC (1951-1969)
Club Colours: Shirts - Maroon & Sky Blue
Shorts - White
Ground Address: Tennant Park, Skewen, Nr. Neath, West Glamorgan
Telephone Nº: None
Ground Capacity: 3,000
Seating Capacity: None
Contact Address: Bob Smith, 50 Southall Avenue, Skewen, Nr. Neath, West Glamorgan
Contact Phone Nº: (0792) 814518

TAFF'S WELL FC
Abacus Division Two

Year Founded: 1947
Nickname: -
Former Names: -
Club Colours: Shirts - Yellow
Shorts - Blue
Ground Address: Rhiw'r Oda, Hillside Park, Taffs Well, Mid Glamorgan
Telephone Nº: (0222) 811080
Ground Capacity: -
Seating Capacity: -
Contact Address: Mr. R. Toghill, 38 Heol Berry, Gwaelod-y-Garth, Taff's Well, Cardiff
Contact Phone Nº: (0222) 811356

TONYREFAIL WELFARE AFC

Abacus Division Two

Year Founded: 1946
Nickname: None
Former Names: None
Club Colours: Shirts - Red with Black Stripe
                Shorts - Black (Red Socks)
Ground Address: Welfare Park, Tonyrefail, Nr. Porth, Rhondda, Mid Glamorgan
Telephone Nº: (0443) 670387 (after Matches)
Ground Capacity: 1,500
Seating Capacity: 100
Contact Address: Mr. P. Jones (Secretary), 13 Rees Street, Treorchy, Rhondda, Mid Glam   CF42 6PL
Contact Phone Nº: (0443) 773460

TREOWEN STARS AFC

Abacus Division Two

Year Founded: 1926
Nickname: None
Former Names: None
Club Colours: Shirts - Blue & White Stripes
                Shorts - Black
Ground Address: Bush Park, Upplands, Newbridge, Gwent
Telephone Nº: (0495) 248249
Ground Capacity: 700
Seating Capacity: None
Contact Address: A. Davies, 19 Meredith Terrace, Newbridge, Gwent
Contact Phone Nº: (0495) 245494

ABERCYNON ATHLETIC FC

Abacus Division Three

Year Founded: 1933
Nickname: None
Former Names: None
Club Colours: Shirts - Black & White
                Shorts - Black
Ground Address: Parc Abercynon, Abercynon, Mid Glamorgan
Telephone Nº: (0443) 238
Ground Capacity: 2,000
Seating Capacity: None
Contact Address: Jeffrey Dudley, 131 Abercynon Road, Abercynon, Mid Glamorgan   CF45 4LU
Contact Phone Nº: (0443) 741433

ALBION ROVERS FC

Abacus Division Three

Year Founded: -
Nickname: -
Former Names: -
Club Colours: Shirts - Red
                Shorts - Red
Ground Address: Crindau Park, Newport, Gwent
Telephone Nº: -
Ground Capacity: -
Seating Capacity: -
Contact Address: c/o Ground
Contact Phone Nº: -

CARDIFF INSTITUTE H.E. FC

Abacus Division Three

Year Founded: 1957
Nickname: -
Former Names: -
Club Colours: Shirts - Maroon & Gold Stripes
Shorts - Maroon
Ground Address: Cyncoed College, Cyncoed Road, Cardiff
Telephone Nº: (0222) 757223
Ground Capacity: -
Seating Capacity: -
Contact Address: Miss K. Smith, 55 Maeshendre, Waunfawr, Aberystwyth, Dyfed   SY23 3PS
Contact Phone Nº: (0970) 612299

GOYTRE UNITED FC

Abacus Division Three

Year Founded: 1963
Nickname: 'Goyts'
Former Names: None
Club Colours: Shirts - Blue & White
Shorts - Blue
Ground Address: Glenhavod Park, Goytre, Port Talbot, West Glamorgan
Telephone Nº: (0639) 898983
Ground Capacity: 4,000
Seating Capacity: 213
Contact Address: B. Suhanski, 20 Goytre Crescent, Goytre, Port Talbot, West Glamorgan
Contact Phone Nº: (0639) 886826

GRANGE HARLEQUINS FC

Abacus Division Three

Year Founded: -
Nickname: -
Former Names: -
Club Colours: Shirts - Red
Shorts - White
Ground Address: Jubilee Park, Sloper Road, Grangetown, Cardiff
Telephone Nº: None
Ground Capacity: -
Seating Capacity: -
Contact Address: Mr. M. Smith-Phillips, 48 Penlan Road, Llandough, Penarth, CF6 1LT
Contact Phone Nº: (0222) 700200

PANTEG AFC

Abacus Division Three

Year Founded: 1940
Nickname: 'Teg'
Former Names: Griffithstown FC
Club Colours: Shirts - Black & White Stripes
Shorts - Black (Black Socks)
Ground Address: Panteg House, Greenhill Road, Griffithstown, Pontypool, Gwent
Telephone Nº: (0495) 763605
Ground Capacity: 5,000
Seating Capacity: None
Contact Address: Bob Small (Club Secretary), 24 Laburnum Drive, New Inn, Pontypool
Contact Phone Nº: (0495) 756280

PENRHIWCEIBER RANGERS FC

Year Founded: 1961
Nickname: None
Former Names: Penrhiwceiber Welfare FC
Club Colours: Shirts - Red
                    Shorts - Red
Ground Address: Glasbrook Field, Glasbrook Terrace, Penrhiwceiber, Mountain Ash, Mid Glam.
Telephone Nº: None
Ground Capacity: 3,000
Seating Capacity: 300
Contact Address: Chris Kerr, 8 Church Street, Penrhiwceiber, Mountain Ash, Mid Glamorgan
Contact Phone Nº: 476134

PONTARDAWE ATHLETIC FC

Year Founded: 1947
Nickname: None
Former Names: None
Club Colours: Shirts - Blue & White Stripes
                    Shorts - Black
Ground Address: The Recreation Ground, Pontardawe
Telephone Nº: (0792) 862228
Ground Capacity: -
Seating Capacity: None
Contact Address: c/o 123 Swansea Road, Trebanos, Pontardawe
Contact Phone Nº: (0792) 865538

PONTLOTTYN BLAST FURNACE AFC

Year Founded: 1968
Nickname: 'The Blast'
Former Names: None
Club Colours: Shirts - Yellow
                    Shorts - Black
Ground Address: Welfare Ground, Hill Road, Pontlottyn
Telephone Nº: None
Ground Capacity: 5,000
Seating Capacity: None
Contact Address: Secretary, "Wordesley", Gwerthonor Road, Gilfach, Bargoed   CF8 8JS
Contact Phone Nº: (0443) 831606

PORT TYWYN SUBURBS FC

Year Founded: -
Nickname: -
Former Names: -
Club Colours: Shirts -
                    Shorts -
Ground Address: -
Telephone Nº: -
Ground Capacity: -
Seating Capacity: -
Contact Address: -
Contact Phone Nº: -

SOUTH WALES CONSTABULARY FC Abacus Division Three

Year Founded: 1969
Nickname: -
Former Names: -
Club Colours: Shirts - Red & Blue
            Shorts - Blue
Ground Address: Athletic Ground, Waterton Cross, Bridgend, Mid Glamorgan
Telephone Nº: (0656) 655555 ext. 2766
Ground Capacity: -
Seating Capacity: -
Contact Address: Mr. A. Davies, 147 Bwlch Road, Fairwater, Cardiff   CF5 3EE
Contact Phone Nº: (0222) 569105

AFC TONDU Abacus Division Three

Year Founded: 1898
Nickname: 'The Robins'
Former Names: Tondu Robins FC
Club Colours: Shirts - Red
            Shorts - Black
Ground Address: Pandy Park, Aberkenfig
Telephone Nº: None
Ground Capacity: -
Seating Capacity: None
Contact Address: c/o Tondu Cricket Club, Bryn Road, Tondu
Contact Phone Nº: (0656) 720045

TREHARRIS ATHLETIC AFC Abacus Division Three

Year Founded: 1889
Nickname: 'The Lilywhites'
Former Names: None
Club Colours: Shirts - Blue & White Stripe
            Shorts - Royal Blue
Ground Address: Commercial Terrace, Treharris, Mid Glamorgan
Telephone Nº: None
Ground Capacity: 1,500
Seating Capacity: None
Contact Address: Mike Casey (Sec.), 10 Windsor Road, Edwardsville, Treharris, Mid Glam CF46 5NP
Contact Phone Nº: (0443) 411153

TRELEWIS AFC Abacus Division Three

Year Founded: 1966
Nickname: None
Former Names: None
Club Colours: Shirts - White with Red Trim
            Shorts - Red
Ground Address: Trelewis Welfare Ground, Brondeg, Trelewis, Treharris, Mid Glamorgan
Telephone Nº: None
Ground Capacity: 400
Seating Capacity: None
Contact Address: John T. Toner (Sec.), 12 Willow Rise, Penpedairheol, Hengoed, Mid Glam CF8 8DR
Contact Phone Nº: (0443) 835078

BUCKLEY TOWN FC
Read Construction Premier Division

Year Founded: 1948
Nickname: 'Wanderers'
Former Names: Buckley Rovers FC, Buckley Wanderers FC
Club Colours: Shirts - Amber
Shorts - Black
Ground Address: Hawksbury, Buckley, Clwyd
Telephone Nº: (0244) 546893
Ground Capacity: 1,000
Seating Capacity: None
Contact Address: c/o 4 Hillary Grove, Buckley, Clwyd
Contact Phone Nº: (0244) 546893

CASTELL ALUN COLTS FC
Read Construction Premier Division

Year Founded: -
Nickname: 'Colts'
Former Names: -
Club Colours: Shirts - Yellow & Green
Shorts - Green
Ground Address: Castell Alun School, Hope
Telephone Nº: -
Ground Capacity: -
Seating Capacity: -
Contact Address: -
Contact Phone Nº: -

CHIRK A.A.A. FC
Read Construction Premier Division

Year Founded: 1875
Nickname: None
Former Names: None
Club Colours: Shirts - Blue and Black Stripes
Shorts - Black
Ground Address: Hollyhead Road, Chirk, Nr. Wrexham, Clwyd
Telephone Nº: (0691) 773676
Ground Capacity: -
Seating Capacity: None
Contact Address: Nigel Roberts (Secretary), 10 Fernhill Avenue, Gobowen, Oswestry, Shropshire
Contact Phone Nº: (0691) 650617

CORWEN AMATEURS FC
Read Construction Premier Division

Year Founded: 1921
Nickname: 'Reds'
Former Names: Corwen Rangers FC
Club Colours: Shirts - Red and White
Shorts - Red
Ground Address: War Memorial Park, Green Lane, Corwen, Clwyd
Telephone Nº: None
Ground Capacity: -
Seating Capacity: None
Contact Address: c/o Gwyneryn, The Crescent, Corwen, Clwyd
Contact Phone Nº: (0490) 412605

LEX XI RESERVES
Read Construction Premier Division

Year Founded: 1965
Nickname: -
Former Names: -
Club Colours: Shirts - Amber
Shorts - Black
Ground Address: Stansty Park, Mold Road, Wrexham
Telephone Nº: (0978) 262129
Ground Capacity: 500
Seating Capacity: None
Contact Address: P.L. Jones, 18 Mayflower Drive, Marford, Wrexham
Contact Phone Nº: (0978) 854028

LLAY ROYAL BRITISH LEGION FC
Read Construction Premier

Year Founded: 1972
Nickname: 'The Legion'
Former Names: -
Club Colours: Shirts - Sky Blue & Royal Blue
Shorts - Royal Blue
Ground Address: Nant-Y-Gaer Road, Llay, Wrexham, Clwyd
Telephone Nº: None
Ground Capacity: -
Seating Capacity: -
Contact Address: Mr. G. Crewe, 17 Trewern Close, Llay, Wrexham, Clwyd   LL12 0RP
Contact Phone Nº: (0978) 855402

LLAY WELFARE FC
Read Construction Premier Division

Year Founded: 1932
Nickname: 'The Welfare'
Former Names: None
Club Colours: Shirts - Black & White Stripes
Shorts - White
Ground Address: Llay Miners Welfare Institute, The Ring, Llay, Nr. Wrexham, Clwyd
Telephone Nº: (0978) 853686
Ground Capacity: -
Seating Capacity: None
Contact Address: S.J. Davies, 6 Sandrock Road, Marford, Nr. Wrexham   LL12 8LT
Contact Phone Nº: (0978) 854429

MARCHWIEL VILLA FC
Read Construction Premier Division

Year Founded: 1984
Nickname: 'The Lions'
Former Names: None
Club Colours: Shirts - White
Shorts - Blue
Ground Address: Station Road, Marchwiel, Nr. Wrexham, Clwyd
Telephone Nº: None
Ground Capacity: 150
Seating Capacity: None
Contact Address: Howard Lloyd, 39 Piercy Avenue, Marchwiel, Wrexham, Clwyd   LL12 0RL
Contact Phone Nº: (0978) 262419

NEW BROUGHTON FC

Read Construction Premier Division

Year Founded: 1986
Nickname: None
Former Names: None
Club Colours: Shirts - Red
Shorts - Black
Ground Address: The Recreation Ground, New Broughton, Nr. Wrexham, Clwyd
Telephone Nº: None
Ground Capacity: -
Seating Capacity: None
Contact Address: c/o 33 Barons Road, Wrexham, Clwyd   LL13 8HB
Contact Phone Nº: (0978) 365454

OVERTON ATHLETIC FC

Read Construction Premier Division

Year Founded: 1970
Nickname: None
Former Names: Overton St. Marys FC
Club Colours: Shirts - Black and Blue Stripes
Shorts - Black
Ground Address: Wrexham Road, Overton-On-Dee, Nr. Wrexham, Clwyd
Telephone Nº: None
Ground Capacity: 500
Seating Capacity: None
Contact Address: c/o 87 The Meadows, Stansty Gardens, Gwersyllt, Nr. Wrexham, Clwyd
Contact Phone Nº: (0978) 752301

PENYCAE FC

Read Construction Premier Division

Year Founded: 1982 (Reformed)
Nickname: 'The Cae'
Former Names: None
Club Colours: Shirts - Royal Blue
Shorts - Royal Blue
Ground Address: Afoneitha Road, Penycae, Nr. Wrexham, Clwyd
Telephone Nº: None
Ground Capacity: 400
Seating Capacity: None
Contact Address: Mr S.M. Griffiths, 35 Chapel Street, Penycae, Nr. Wrexham, Clwyd   LL14 2RF
Contact Phone Nº: (0978) 842967

RUTHIN TOWN FC RESERVES

Read Construction Premier Division

Year Founded: 1951
Nickname: 'The Blues'
Former Names: Ruthin British Legion FC
Club Colours: Shirts - Blue & White
Shorts - Blue
Ground Address: Memorial Playing Fields, Parc-y-Dre, Ruthin, Clwyd
Telephone Nº: (08242) 2766
Ground Capacity: 2,000
Seating Capacity: None
Contact Address: B. Lewis, 40 Maeshafod, Ruthin, Clwyd   LL15 1LS
Contact Phone Nº: (0824) 702828 ?

TREUDDYN VILLA FC

Read Construction Premier Division

Year Founded: -
Nickname: 'Villa'
Former Names: -
Club Colours: Shirts - Red & White Stripes
                   Shorts - Black
Ground Address: Leeswood, Treuddyn
Telephone Nº: -
Ground Capacity: -
Seating Capacity: -
Contact Address: -
Contact Phone Nº: -

CLWB PÊL DROED Y FELINHELI

Sealink Stena Welsh Alliance

Year Founded: 1977
Nickname: 'Felin'
Former Names: Port Dinorwic FC
Club Colours: Shirts - Orange
                   Shorts - Navy Blue
Ground Address: Cae Seilo, Y Felinheli, Gwynedd
Telephone Nº: None
Ground Capacity: 1,000
Seating Capacity: None
Contact Address: Mr E.V. Hughes, Annedd Wen, 38 Stryd Bangor, Y Felinheli, Gwynedd
Contact Phone Nº: (0248) 670359

LLANDYRNOG UNITED FC

Sealink Stena Welsh Alliance

Year Founded: 1975
Nickname: 'Dyrni'
Former Names: None
Club Colours: Shirts - White
                   Shorts - Dark Blue
Ground Address: Cae Nant, Llandyrnog, Denbigh
Telephone Nº: None
Ground Capacity: 500
Seating Capacity: None
Contact Address: Dewi Lewis, Bryn Elwy, Allt Goch, Trefnant, St. Asaph, Clwyd
Contact Phone Nº: (0745) 730378

LLANFAIRPWLL FC

Sealink Stena Welsh Alliance

Year Founded: Late 1890's - Currently reformed 1972
Nickname: None
Former Names: None
Club Colours: Shirts - Blue and Dark Blue Stripes
                   Shorts - Black
Ground Address: Gors Field, Llanfairpwll, Anglesey, Gwynedd
Telephone Nº: None
Ground Capacity: 750 - 1,000
Seating Capacity: None
Contact Address: A.W. Mummery (Sec.), 39 Trem Eryri, Llanfairpwll, Anglesey, Gwynedd LL61 5JF
Contact Phone Nº: (0248) 714938

LLANGEFNI TOWN FC

Sealink Stena Welsh Alliance

Year Founded: 1892
Nickname: None
Former Names: Llangefni FC, Llangefni Albion FC, Llangefni Rovers FC, Llangefni United FC
Club Colours: Shirts - Blue, Red & White
Shorts - Blue
Ground Address: Lon Newydd, Isgraig, Llangefni
Telephone Nº: None
Ground Capacity: 1,500
Seating Capacity: None
Contact Address: Miss Nia Fôn (Secretary), 15 Pencraig, Llangefni
Contact Phone Nº: (0248) 723572

LLANRWST UNITED FC

Sealink Stena Welsh Alliance

Year Founded: 1983
Nickname: 'Roosters'
Former Names: Gwydir Rovers FC, Llanrwst Town FC, Llanrwst Athletic FC
Club Colours: Shirts - Yellow and Red Stripes
Shorts - Red
Ground Address: Gwydir Park, Llanrwst, Gwynedd
Telephone Nº: None
Ground Capacity: -
Seating Capacity: None
Contact Address: Geraint Vaughan-Humphreys (Sec.), 63 Cae Person, Llanrwst, Gwynedd LL26 0HT
Contact Phone Nº: (0492) 642056

LOCOMOTIVE LLANBERIS FC

Sealink Stena Welsh Alliance

Year Founded: 1890
Nickname: 'Darrens'
Former Names: Llanberis Athletic FC
Club Colours: Shirts - Black & Amber
Shorts - Black
Ground Address: Ffordd Padarn, Llanberis, Gwynedd
Telephone Nº: None
Ground Capacity: 1,000
Seating Capacity: None
Contact Address: E. Thomas (Secretary), 9 Stryd-Y-Ffynnon, Llanberis, Gwynedd LL55 4EW
Contact Phone Nº: (0286) 872274

NANTLLE VALE FC

Sealink Stena Welsh Alliance

Year Founded: Not Known
Nickname: 'The Vale'
Former Names: None
Club Colours: Shirts - Blue and White
Shorts -Blue
Ground Address: Maes Dulyn, Penygroes, Caernarfon
Telephone Nº: None
Ground Capacity: 3,000
Seating Capacity: 200
Contact Address: Mrs H. Roberts, "Gwynfa", Ffordd Rhedyw, Llanllyfni, Caernarfon LL54 6SG
Contact Phone Nº: (0286) 881139

NEFYN UNITED FC
Sealink Stena Welsh Alliance

Year Founded: 1950
Nickname: 'The Herrings'
Former Names: Nefyn Celts FC
Club Colours: Shirts - Blue
Shorts - Blue
Ground Address: Cae'r Delyn, Nefyn, Pwllheli
Telephone Nº: (0758) 720027
Ground Capacity: 500
Seating Capacity: None
Contact Address: c/o Cwr Y Coed, Nefyn, Pwllheli
Contact Phone Nº: (0758) 720027

PENMAENMAWR PHOENIX FC
Sealink Stena Welsh Alliance

Year Founded: 1973
Nickname: 'Yellow Boys'
Former Names: Penmaenmawr FC
Club Colours: Shirts - Yellow
Shorts - Blue
Ground Address: Cae Bron Wylfa, Conwy Road, Penmaenmawr, Gwynedd
Telephone Nº: None
Ground Capacity: -
Seating Capacity: None
Contact Address: Secretary, 13 Maes Alltwen, Penmaenmawr, Gwynedd   LL34 6UA
Contact Phone Nº: (0492) 623435

PILKINGTONS - ST. ASAPH
Sealink Stena Welsh Alliance

Year Founded: 1965
Nickname: -
Former Names: -
Club Colours: Shirts - Green & White Stripes
Shorts - Black
Ground Address: Glascoed Road Sports Ground, Glascoed Road, St. Asaph
Telephone Nº: (0745) 528458
Ground Capacity: -
Seating Capacity: -
Contact Address: S. Pender, 15 Maes Hedydd, Rhyl, Clwyd   LL18 4RW
Contact Phone Nº: -

RHYDYMWYN FC
Sealink Stena Welsh Alliance

Year Founded: 1910
Nickname: None
Former Names: None
Club Colours: Shirts - Yellow
Shorts - Black
Ground Address: Recreation Ground, Denbigh Road, Rhydymwyn, Nr. Mold
Telephone Nº: None
Ground Capacity: -
Seating Capacity: None
Contact Address: M. Ratcliffe, 33 Llys Y Wern, Sychoyh, Nr. Mold, Clwyd   CH7 6BJ
Contact Phone Nº: (0352) 757161

BARRY TOWN FC RESERVES
Highadmit Projects Amateur League

Year Founded: 1912
Nickname: 'Linnetts'
Former Names: Barri Town FC
Club Colours: Shirts - Green
Shorts - Blue
Ground Address: Jenner Park, Barry, South Glamorgan   CF6 7BG
Telephone Nº: -
Ground Capacity: 5,000
Seating Capacity: 1,600
Contact Address: A Whelan, 166 Jenner Road, Barry, South Glamorgan
Contact Phone Nº: (0446) 737188

BETTWS ATHLETIC FC
Highadmit Projects Amateur League

Year Founded: -
Nickname: -
Former Names: -
Club Colours: Shirts - Red
Shorts - Blue
Ground Address: Bettws Playing Fields, Bettws, Bridgend, Mid Glamorgan
Telephone Nº: -
Ground Capacity: -
Seating Capacity: -
Contact Address: S. Jones, 60 Maes Talcen, Brackla, Bridgend, Mid Glamorgan
Contact Phone Nº: (0656) 663396

B.P. BARRY FC
Highadmit Projects Amateur League

Year Founded: 1991 (1969)
Nickname: 'Islanders'
Former Names: Dow Corning FC
Club Colours: Shirts - Black & White Stripes
Shorts - Black
Ground Address: B.P. Sports & Social Club, Swanbridge, Sully, Nr. Barry, South Glamorgan
Telephone Nº: (0222) 530629
Ground Capacity: -
Seating Capacity: None
Contact Address: c/o 6 Carmarthen Close, Barry, South Glamorgan   CF8 7AS
Contact Phone Nº: (0446) 741044

CEFN CRIBWR BOYS' CLUB FC
Highadmit Amateur League

Year Founded: 1976
Nickname: None
Former Names: None
Club Colours: Shirts - Blue with White Trim
Shorts - Blue with White Trim
Ground Address: Cae Gof Playing Fields, Cefn Cribwr, Bridgend, Mid Glamorgan
Telephone Nº: (0656) 743613
Ground Capacity: -
Seating Capacity: None
Contact Address: c/o 2 Woodlands Park, Kenfig Hill, Bridgend, Mid Glamorgan   CF33 6DY
Contact Phone Nº: (0656) 743613

COGAN CORONATION JUNIORS FC   Highadmit Amateur League

Year Founded: -
Nickname: None
Former Names: Cogan St. Patricks FC
Club Colours: Shirts - Green
               Shorts - White
Ground Address: Cogan Recreation Ground, Cogan, Penarth, South Glamorgan
Telephone Nº: None
Ground Capacity: -
Seating Capacity: None
Contact Address: c/o 2 Chantry Rise, Penarth, South Glamorgan   CF6 2BS
Contact Phone Nº: (0222) 706132

GRANGE ALBION AFC   Highadmit Projects Amateur League

Year Founded: 1943
Nickname: None
Former Names: None
Club Colours: Shirts - Black & White Stripes
               Shorts - Black
Ground Address: Coronation Park, Sloper Road, Grangetown, Cardiff
Telephone Nº: None
Ground Capacity: -
Seating Capacity: None
Contact Address: Mr. N. Dimond, 7 Ystrad Street, Grangetown, Cardiff   CF1 7AH
Contact Phone Nº: (0222) 231868

LES CROUPIERS CAERAU FC (ELY)   Highadmit Amateur League

Year Founded: -
Nickname: -
Former Names: -
Club Colours: Shirts - Red
               Shorts - Black
Ground Address: Glynderw School Field
Telephone Nº: -
Ground Capacity: -
Seating Capacity: -
Contact Address: J. Jarvis, 326 Cowbridge Road West, Ely, Cardiff   CF5 5BY
Contact Phone Nº: (0222) 591969

LISVANE-HEATH HORNETS FC   Highadmit Amateur League

Year Founded: 1989   (Heath Hornets FC founded 1965, Lisvane FC founded 1979)
Nickname: 'The Hornets'
Former Names: The current club was formed by a merger of Heath Hornets FC and Lisvane FC in 1989
Club Colours: Shirts - Tangerine
               Shorts - Navy Blue
Ground Address: The Village Field, Heol-Y-Delyn, Lisvane, Cardiff
Telephone Nº: None
Ground Capacity: 500
Seating Capacity: None
Contact Address: E.M. Dobie, 20 Heol-Y-Delyn, Lisvane, Cardiff   CF4 5SQ
Contact Phone Nº: (0222) 757652

LLWYDCOED WELFARE FC

Year Founded: 1948
Nickname: 'The Coed'
Former Names: Llwydcoed Boys Club FC
Club Colours:　Shirts - Black & White Stripes
　　　　　　　　　Shorts -Black
Ground Address: Merthyr Road, Llwydcoed, Aberdare, Mid Glamorgan　CF44 0YA
Telephone Nº: 874514
Ground Capacity: 500
Seating Capacity: None
Contact Address: As Ground Address
Contact Phone Nº: -

PENBRYN & DISTRICT FC

Year Founded: -
Nickname: -
Former Names: -
Club Colours:　Shirts - Blue & Yellow
　　　　　　　　　Shorts - Black
Ground Address: Cefn Llwynau, Penbryn
Telephone Nº: --
Ground Capacity: -
Seating Capacity: -
Contact Address: -
Contact Phone Nº: -

STANLEYTOWN FC

Year Founded: -
Nickname: -
Former Names: -
Club Colours:　Shirts - Red
　　　　　　　　　Shorts - Black
Ground Address: Stanleytown Playing Fields, Stanleytown, Rhondda
Telephone Nº: -
Ground Capacity: -
Seating Capacity: -
Contact Address: C. Rowlands, 3A Middle Terrace, Stanleytown, Rhondda　CF43 3ET
Contact Phone Nº: -

ST. JOSEPH'S FC

Year Founded: -
Nickname: -
Former Names: -
Club Colours:　Shirts - Gold
　　　　　　　　　Shorts - Black
Ground Address: Blackweir
Telephone Nº: -
Ground Capacity: -
Seating Capacity: -
Contact Address: -
Contact Phone Nº: -

TONGWYNLAIS FC

Year Founded: 1935
Nickname: 'The Ton'
Former Names: None
Club Colours: Shirts - Red
                 Shorts - Black
Ground Address: Ironbridge Road, Tongwynlais
Telephone Nº: (0222) 342985
Ground Capacity: Over 300
Seating Capacity: None
Contact Address: c/o 7 Harriet Street, Cathays, Cardiff   CF2 4BU
Contact Phone Nº: As Above

TREDOMEN AFC

Year Founded: 1921
Nickname: 'The Engineers'
Former Names: None
Club Colours: Shirts - Black & Red Stripes
                 Shorts - Black
Ground Address: Athletic Stadium, Ystrad Mynach, Hengoed, Mid Glamorgan
Telephone Nº: (0443) 814327 (Club)
Ground Capacity: 1,000
Seating Capacity: None
Contact Address: c/o 12 Tyn-Y-Coed, Ystrad Mynach, Hengoed, Mid Glamorgan
Contact Phone Nº: (0443) 812784

TRELAI YOUTH CLUB FC

Year Founded: 1970
Nickname: None
Former Names: None
Club Colours: Shirts - White
                 Shorts - Navy Blue
Ground Address: Bishopston Road, Ely, Cardiff
Telephone Nº: (0222) 566106
Ground Capacity: 200
Seating Capacity: None
Contact Address: c/o 54 Riverside Terrace, Ely, Cardiff
Contact Phone Nº: (0222) 566234

WENVOE PARK FC

Year Founded: -
Nickname: -
Former Names: -
Club Colours: Shirts - Green & Yellow
                 Shorts - Green & Yellow
Ground Address: Station Road, Wenvoe
Telephone Nº: -
Ground Capacity: -
Seating Capacity: -
Contact Address: S. Fowler, 7 Andover Close, Highlight Park, Barry, South Glamorgan
Contact Phone Nº: (0446) 749786

ABERYSTWYTH TOWN FC RES.

Year Founded: 1884
Nickname: 'Seasiders'
Former Names: Aberystwyth FC
Club Colours: Shirts - Green & Black
                            Shorts - Black
Ground Address: Park Avenue, Aberystwyth, Dyfed
Telephone Nº: (0970) 612122
Ground Capacity: 2,500
Seating Capacity: 250
Contact Address: A.O. Griffiths, Boar's Head, Queen's Road, Aberystwyth, Dyfed   SY23 2HT
Contact Phone Nº: (0970) 626106

BERRIEW FC

Year Founded: 1883
Nickname: 'Black-Ambers'
Former Names: None
Club Colours: Shirts - Amber
                            Shorts - Black
Ground Address: Thomas Lant Fields, Pendre, Builth Wells, Powys
Telephone Nº: None
Ground Capacity: 3,000
Seating Capacity: 160
Contact Address: M.L. Jones, Bryncoed, 8 Iron Bridge Road, Builth Wells, Powys
Contact Phone Nº: (0982) 553673

BUILTH WELLS FC

Year Founded: 1883
Nickname: 'Black-Ambers'
Former Names: None
Club Colours: Shirts - Amber
                            Shorts - Black
Ground Address: Thomas Lant Fields, Pendre, Builth Wells, Powys
Telephone Nº: None
Ground Capacity: 3,000
Seating Capacity: 160
Contact Address: M.L. Jones, Bryncoed, 8 Irfon Bridge Road, Builth Wells, Powys
Contact Phone Nº: (0982) 553673

CAERSWS FC RESERVES

Year Founded: 1887
Nickname: 'Blue Birds'
Former Names: Caersws Amateurs FC
Club Colours: Shirts - Blue
                            Shorts - White
Ground Address: Recreation Ground, Caersws, Powys
Telephone Nº: (0686) 688753
Ground Capacity: 3,000
Seating Capacity: 150
Contact Address: T.M.B. Jones, 3 Hafren Terrace, Caersws, Powys
Contact Phone Nº: (0686) 688103

CLUN VALLEY FC

Year Founded: 1890
Nickname: -
Former Names: -
Club Colours: Shirts - Yellow
Shorts - Blue
Ground Address: The Playing Fields, Clun
Telephone Nº: -
Ground Capacity: -
Seating Capacity: None
Contact Address: M. B. Rosser, Bonnavista, Newcastle, Craven Arms, Shropshire
Contact Phone Nº: (0588) 640562

KINGTON TOWN FC

Year Founded: 1880
Nickname: -
Former Names: -
Club Colours: Shirts - Yellow
Shorts - Black
Ground Address: Mill Street, Kington, Powys
Telephone Nº: (0544) 231007
Ground Capacity: -
Seating Capacity: 100
Contact Address: K. Gwynne, 8 Perserverance Close, Kington, Hereford
Contact Phone Nº: (0544) 230845

KNIGHTON FC RESERVES

Year Founded: 1881
Nickname: 'Town'
Former Names: -
Club Colours: Shirts - Red
Shorts - White
Ground Address: Bryn Y Castell, Knighton, Powys
Telephone Nº: (0547) 528999
Ground Capacity: 2,000
Seating Capacity: 50
Contact Address: Mrs. C.A. Sutton, "Ashdown", 1 Underhill Crescent, Knighton, Powys   LD7 1DG
Contact Phone Nº: (0547) 528953

LLANDRINDOD WELLS FC

Year Founded: 1883
Nickname: 'Blues'
Former Names: None
Club Colours: Shirts - Blue and White
Shorts - White
Ground Address: 'Broadway', Lant Avenue, Llandrindod Wells, Powys
Telephone Nº: (0597) 823030
Ground Capacity: 2,000
Seating Capacity: 250
Contact Address: Paul Watkins (Secretary), Camelot, Hillcrest Drive, Llandrindod Wells   LD1 5DG
Contact Phone Nº: (0597) 823517

LLANSANTFFRAID FC RESERVES

Richards the Builders League

Year Founded: 1959
Nickname: 'Saints'
Former Names: None
Club Colours: Shirts - Green
                Shorts - Black
Ground Address: Recreation Ground, Treflan, Llansantffraid, Powys
Telephone Nº: (0691) 828112
Ground Capacity: 1,500
Seating Capacity: 130
Contact Address: G.M.G. Ellis, Brodawel, Church Lane, Llansantffraid, Powys   SY22 6AP
Contact Phone Nº: (0691) 828583

MACHYNLLETH TOWN FC

Richards the Builders League

Year Founded: 1885
Nickname: 'The Maglonians'
Former Names: None
Club Colours: Shirts - Blue & White Quarters
                Shorts - Blue
Ground Address: Cae-Glas, Plas Grounds, Machynlleth, Powys
Telephone Nº: (0654) 702734
Ground Capacity: Not Known
Seating Capacity: None
Contact Address: c/o 4 Treowain, Machynlleth, Powys   SY20 8EH
Contact Phone Nº: (0654) 702734

MORDA UNITED FC

Richards the Builders League

Year Founded: 1897 (Folded 1954)   Reformed in 1976
Nickname: 'Blues'
Former Names: Morda FC
Club Colours: Shirts - Royal Blue
                Shorts -Yellow (Blue Socks)
Ground Address: Weston Road, Morda, Oswestry, Shropshire
Telephone Nº: (0691) 659621 (Morda Social Club)
Ground Capacity: Approximately 1,500
Seating Capacity: 116
Contact Address: Mike Clarke (Secretary), 50 Langland Road, Oswestry, Shropshire
Contact Phone Nº: (0691) 661985

NEWTOWN FC RESERVES

Richards the Builders League

Year Founded: 1875
Nickname: 'The Robins'
Former Names: Newtown Whitestars FC
Club Colours: Shirts - Red
                Shorts - White
Ground Address: Latham Park, Newtown, Powys
Telephone Nº: (0686) 626159
Ground Capacity: 5,000
Seating Capacity: 220
Contact Address: K. Harding, 7 Tradyddan Terrace, Newtown, Powys   SY16 2ER
Contact Phone Nº: (0686) 628523

PENPARCAU FC

Year Founded: 1983
Nickname: -
Former Names: -
Club Colours: Shirts - Black & White Stripe
Shorts - Black
Ground Address: Min Y Ddol Playing Fields, Penparcau, Aberystwyth
Telephone Nº: None
Ground Capacity: -
Seating Capacity: None
Contact Address: M. Gilbert, 19 Penrheidol, Penparcau, Aberystwyth, Dyfed   SY23 1QW
Contact Phone Nº: (0970) 617324

PENRHYNCOCH FC RESERVES

Year Founded: 1965
Nickname: None
Former Names: None
Club Colours: Shirts - Yellow
Shorts - Blue
Ground Address: Cae Baker, Penrhyncoch, Aberystwyth, Dyfed
Telephone Nº: (0970) 828992
Ground Capacity: -
Seating Capacity: None
Contact Address: R.J. Ellis, 4 Maes Laura, Aberystwyth, Dyfed   SY23 2AU
Contact Phone Nº:

PRESTEIGNE ST. ANDREWS FC

Year Founded: 1897
Nickname: 'The Saints'
Former Names: None
Club Colours: Shirts - Black with Red Stripe
Shorts - Black
Ground Address: Llanandras Park, Clatterbrune, Presteigne, Powys   LD8
Telephone Nº: (0544) 207838
Ground Capacity: 2,000
Seating Capacity: 150
Contact Address: Mrs D.M. Field, 14 Orchard Close, Presteigne, Powys
Contact Phone Nº: (0544) 260085

TALGARTH AFC

Year Founded: Reformed 1969
Nickname: None
Former Names: None
Club Colours: Shirts - Yellow, White & Blue
Shorts - Blue, Yellow & White
Ground Address: Kings George V Playing Fields, Westfields, Talgarth
Telephone Nº: (0874) 711765
Ground Capacity: -
Seating Capacity: None
Contact Address: Mrs J. Berry, 3 The Terrace, Trefecca, Talgarth
Contact Phone Nº: (0874) 711765

VALE OF ARROW FC

Richards the Builders League

Year Founded: 1948
Nickname: None
Former Names: None
Club Colours: Shirts - Navy Blue & White Stripes
                    Shorts - Navy Blue
Ground Address: Cae Dressy, Gladestry, Kington
Telephone Nº: (0544) 22629
Ground Capacity: -
Seating Capacity: None
Contact Address: c/o Burnt House, Gladestry, Kington
Contact Phone Nº: (0544) 22629

WATERLOO ROVERS FC

Richards the Builders League

Year Founded: Reformed 1978
Nickname: None
Former Names: None
Club Colours: Shirts - Red
                    Shorts - Red
Ground Address: Maesydre Recreation Ground, Severn Road, Welshpool, Powys   SY21 7HN
Telephone Nº: None
Ground Capacity: -
Seating Capacity: None
Contact Address: Cllr. Ray Dart, 47 Erw-wen, Welshpool, Powys   SY21 7HN
Contact Phone Nº: (0938) 553698

WELSH FOOTBALL ALMANAC 1991

Edited by Mel ap Ior Thomas, David Collins, Adrian Dumphy
(published 1991)

- **Details of the top clubs in Wales**
- **League results & final tables 1990-91**
- **League Cups & Area Cup results in full**
- **Club Data for 1991-92**
- **Lists of Past winners of Leagues & Cups**
- **Allbright Bitter Welsh Cup results 1990-91**
- **List of past finals and final line-ups 1945-1991**
- **Ansells (Wales) Intermediate Cup results 1990-91**
- **List of past finals (including preceding Amateur Cup)**
- **Data on National Team, current squads, etc.**
- **Playing record against foreign opposition with statistical summary of performance**
- **Team line-ups for all 'A' Internationals since 1945**
- **Welsh Clubs in Europe**

Priced only **£4.95** *+ £1.50 postage*
(less than half-price)

Only available from: -   **The Soccer Bookshelf**
72 St. Peter's Avenue
Cleethorpes
South Humberside
DN35 8HU
ENGLAND

Other Supporters' Guides : -

THE SUPPORTERS' GUIDE TO PREMIER & FOOTBALL LEAGUE CLUBS 1994

Featuring :
- all Premier League clubs
- all Football League clubs
- all 3 British National Stadia
+ 1992/93 season's Results & tables

120 pages - price £4.99 - post free

THE SUPPORTERS' GUIDE TO NON-LEAGUE FOOTBALL 1994

Featuring :
- all GM/Vauxhall Conference clubs
- all HFS Loans - Premier clubs
- all Beazer Homes - Premier clubs
- all Diadora Premier clubs
+ 180 other major Non-League clubs

112 pages - price £4.99 - post free

THE SUPPORTERS' GUIDE TO SCOTTISH FOOTBALL 1994

Featuring :
- all Scottish League clubs
- all Highland League clubs
- all East of Scotland League clubs
+ Results, tables

96 pages - price £4.99 - post free

order from : -

**SOCCER BOOK PUBLISHING LTD.
72 ST. PETERS AVENUE
CLEETHORPES
DN35 8HU
ENGLAND**